A Walk Through
LYMINGTON
EDWARD KING

GW00497871

Ensign
PUBLICATIONS

Originally published under the same title in 1972 by Kings of Lymington.

©Kings of Lymington 1972
New, revised edition published in 1990

©David and Janet Irvine 1990
New material, revisions and chapter twelve.
All rights reserved.

Published by Ensign Publications for Kings of Lymington
105/6 High Street, Lymington, Hampshire, SO41 9ZD

Ensign Publications
2 Redcar Street
Southampton SO1 5LL

British Library Cataloguing in Publication Data
King, Edward, 1893-1974
  A walk through Lymington. – 2nd ed.
  1. England, history
  I. Title
  942.275

ISBN 1-85455-056-X

FOREWORD

In providing a revised text for Edward King's book his daughter Janet and son-in-law David Irvine have resisted the temptation to amend or alter the fine, narrative style which has served the book so well since it was first published in 1972. In preference to amendment they have chosen to include more recent information and facts in a series of brief footnotes which appear on the page to which they refer. Hence Edward King's reference to 'twenty' inns on page 4 has been footnoted as 'fourteen' on the same basis as his original assessment in 1972.

Inevitably, over the course of the last eighteen years, a small number of apparently conflicting pieces of evidence have emerged to challenge some of Edward King's original research. It has not been possible to confirm the extent or veracity of these, largely constructive, comments. Certainly a larger number of affirmative recommendations of the book have been confirmed by recent research.

In his own lifetime Edward King was able to prove a number of his own theories about the history of the town he loved. One of the vexed questions was, and to an extent still is, the relative positions of the town halls which were, in turn, built and pulled down in the High Street. Edward King was able to confirm exactly the position of the third town hall, which stood opposite Kings Bookshop, by the simple expedient of standing over the roadmen as they worked on the carriageway. He also attempted to get the known position of this town hall marked with metal studs which would have shown through the surface. Alas his advice went unheeded so the debate continues today.

Of particular interest to local historians and general readers is the new chapter twelve. This text, prepared from a paper Edward King gave to the Historical Record Society in October 1959, gives the reader a chance to explore the history of a distinguished bookselling family.

The printing division of Kings, which incidentally produced the first edition of this book, was sold in 1976 but continued at 105/6 High Street until the new proprietors relocated the business in 1981.

Edward King died in 1974 aged 81. His elder daughter Mary carried on the family bookselling tradition until her untimely death in 1987, just months before her scheduled retirement, and the transfer and sale of the business to a consortium of senior staff in February 1988.

Kings of Lymington could therefore claim, quite rightly, to be the oldest established bookselling business in Britain – being under family control and ownership for over 250 years.

The Publishers

The third Town Hall built in 1720 to impress the Burrard's wealthy friends. It stood opposite Kings bookshop at 105/6 High Street.

CONTENTS

Chapter   Page

1   **A Brief History.** The First Charter. The Courts Leet.
        Government under the Charters. The River. The Three Town
        Halls.   1

2   **A Walk Through Lymington.**   5

3   **Parliamentary Representation.** A Parliamentary Election of
        1832.   19

4   **Memorandum.** The Trade of Lymington by W. Towsey.   23

5   **The Manufacture of Salt.**   27

6   **The Poor House.**   29

7   **Travel in the 18th Century.** Waggons. Coaches and Post-
        chaises. Stage Waggons. Roads, Tolls etc. Inns.   57

8   **The Local Emigrants.**   63

9   **The Church.** The Parish Church. The Vestry Accounts
        Beginning 1669.   69

10   **I Remember.**   95

11   **The Inns of Lymington.**   102

12   **Kings of Lymington.** The Story of an Old Business.   114

The first Town Hall probably dated from 1463. It would appear to have stood on the south side of the High Street on the site of the present numbers 30 and 31.

The second Town Hall. Built in 1684 at a cost to the town of £20. It stood in the High Street at the corner of New Lane.

CHAPTER ONE

A Brief History

The first mention of Lymington in recorded history is in Domesday Book, where the town (or village) is named Lentune. We may however be certain that the town is very much older than this. From its situation, at the lowest point at which the river could be forded, and also at the first practicable landing which would be found by a vessel entering the river, there was probably a settlement here from the earliest times.

The first part of the name of Lymington is Celtic in origin, (the Saxon "ton" must have been added later), and the ancient British camp of Buckland Rings was doubtless built to guard the Port. It is known that this camp was occupied by the Romans (in 18th century nearly 200 pounds weight of Roman coins were discovered here), and some historians think that the Lymington River is the "River Alainus" where the Roman General Aulus Platius landed in A.D. 43. But in this short account we must forego the older history of the town, and carry the reader on to about the time of the Norman conquest, when the town of Lymington was a very small village comprising a cluster of houses at the Quayside and in Gosport Street. Close by at Woodside was a farm of 120 acres, occupied by one Fulcuin, and in the view of the Domesday book assessors this farm was of more value than the village!

The Manor of Lymington, which took its name from the town which it enclosed and was co-extensive in area with the present parish, was created at the Conquest, and was given, with other Manors including that of Christchurch, (Twynham), to Earl Roger of Shrewsbury. It is probable that the salt works, which afterwards made Lymington so valuable a possession, were created at this time, although the first mention of Salterns at Lymington is in a grant of tithes to Quarr Abbey dated 1147. Earl Roger was succeeded by his son, Hugh, who died in 1098; he in turn was succeeded by his brother, Robert, who in 1120 suffered forfeiture of his possessions which were granted to Richard de Redvers, 1st Earl of Devon, subsequently succeeded by his son Baldwin, and his family remained the feudal lords of Lymington until the time of Henry VIII.

THE FIRST CHARTER

In 1150, Baldwin de Redvers, 2nd Earl of Devon, granted us our first Charter, one of the earliest in the Kingdom. The Town was in an outlying corner of his domain, not easily defended by its Lord, and in granting the Burgesses their freedom he imposed on them the onerous duty of their own defence, no light task in those troubled times.

This Charter freed the inhabitants from all tolls and levies to their feudal Lord, in return for which they were to pay him a fixed quit rent. The Borough at this time comprised only the lower part of the town, but about the end of the twelth century William de Redvers (the 16th Earl) granted another Charter which extended the Borough as far as the Church, and this second Charter was confirmed by Baldwin (the 8th Earl) in 1251. No alteration has ever been made by the Crown, Lymington being one of the very few towns in England which has received a Charter from their feudal lord and from him alone.

The boundaries of the Old and New Borough contained about 105 acres. They remained unaltered until the Local Government Act of 1888. The Manor also was then divided into the Manors of Old and New Lymington, but both continued in the same ownership. The extension of the Borough to the Church was known as New Lymington, a name which persisted until quite recent times.

The town officials were the Constables, the Ale taster, the Hayward, the Searchers and Sealers of Leather, and the Meterers or Measurers and Weighers, who usually were collectors also. In later times there was also a Town Clerk and a Town Sergeant. All these officers (except the Town Clerk) were appointed at the Court Leet.

THE COURTS LEET

On the 9th June, 1270, Isabella de Fortibus, the Lady of the Isles, sealed her famous Charter which gave the Burgesses the right to elect their own Mayors (in the place of the Lord's Reeves); each Mayor was presented annually at the Court Leet where he took an oath of allegiance to the Lord of the Manor before a jury of townsmen. This Charter also gave the Court Leet the general supervision of the town's doings during the year; it was also the origin of the river dues and customs. After the passing of the Municipal Corporations Act, 1835, the civil functions of the Court Leet disappeared; until that date the jury acted as a combination of a Magisterial Court and a Sanitary authority.

GOVERNMENT UNDER THE CHARTERS

The town under its Charters was governed by a Mayor and the Burgesses, which latter body at first comprised all the resident householders who paid their share of the town expenses, (scot), and took their turn in watching it, (lot), qualifications which formed the scot and lot voter of a later period. They stood in place of the feudal lord, who had conveyed to them the soil, river, and the quay, with all rights and privileges. Their power and that of the Mayor was much greater than at present: they could for example imprison, more or less at pleasure, for there was no public opinion to check them, and they levied tolls and dues by their own orders.

This system lasted until the passing of the Municipal Corporations Act, 1835. The Burgess Oath shows what were considered the rights and duties of a burgess. In substance it was probably nearly identical at all times.

The earliest Mayor of whom we have record, took office in 1319, that is, in the reign of Edward II; his name was William Lyteltone or Lyteltane and it is stated that one of the first documents he executed was an agreement between the town and the Abbey of Beaulieu (founded about a century before) whereby the abbot agreed to help to defend the town in consideration of being toll free.

THE RIVER

The river was formerly navigable as far as Ampress, where there are remains of river forts. The navigable part was, in olden days, considerably wider, deeper and longer than it is now, and was kept clear by the strong double tides which still rise and fall as far as the bridge. Beyond this the river narrows into what is now an inconsiderable stream called the "Boldre," or full river, a name which was once no doubt appropriate.

In the time of the de Redvers, the Earls, as Lords of the Manor, claimed the whole of the estuary and exacted tolls and dues, and when they gave the Charters to the Burgesses the right to the tolls and dues passed with them.

For many years past the Council have leased the foreshore from the Crown, and now control the river as the Harbour Authority under powers granted by the Lymington River and Harbour Order, 1913.

THE THREE TOWN HALLS

The earliest Town Hall apparently dated from 1463, the fourth year of King Edward IV, when a widow lady residing at Lymington presented to the town a messuage and site, whereon to build one. This Hall was standing after the French burned the town in 1545, and it would appear to have stood on the south side of the High Street on the site of the present Nos. 30 and 31, and the Market Cross was in front in the roadway.

This first Town Hall became in time obsolete and inconvenient, and in 1684 a new one was ordered to be built. The second Town Hall stood opposite the present Nos. 93 and 94 in the High Street, close to the pavement. The pillars from this building are now set up in Woodside Gardens at Lymington.

The third town hall was built in 1720 on an adjoining site. It was a plain structure, on pillars like its predecessors, but with a larger room above. This hall served through the long reigns of the three Georges, down to the middle of the last century. The Market Cross had become ruinous and was removed about 1820; the Town Hall then stood alone, and being in its turn found inconvenient and in the way of carriages and other vehicles, was finally pulled down in 1858 with a great improvement to the street.

C H A P T E R   T W O

A Walk Through Lymington

Lymington has been the home of my family for many generations, so perhaps I am prejudiced in its favour. The very name Lymington has a musical sound and to my mind exactly fits our beautiful town.

It has a certain ill defined charm but I think the fact that there are thirty five bay windows on the first and sometimes the second floors tends to give the town its flavour: something that no other town that I know, has.

Gas Lamps were not introduced till 1830. The only light in the street at night was the odd oil lamp outside the larger houses.

There were forty-five Inns in the town, now there are twenty[1]. In 1776 when Richard Warner, curate to Mr. Gilpin of Boldre, came to Lymington from Basingstoke, it took two days travelling by coach. Four days and three nights away and the private coach cost £5 5s. 0d. Richard Warner wrote "The females of Lymington were at that time almost proverbial for their beauty and it was a general observation among those who visited the place that in no other town in England of a like population were to be found so many females in all ranks and degree of life on whom nature had conferred such personal charms as on the youthful fair of this favoured spot".

Few families had incomes of over £300 per annum.

Travel in olden times was a tedious business. In 1715 when Mr. Trattle our Town Clerk went to Winchester on borough business it took four days going and coming back. To put up at Redbridge (a days journey) cost him 7/10, at Winchester he spent £1 2s. 6d. and returning to Redbridge 6/10. Turnpike gates 2/–. The chaise and driver cost 4/– (remarkably cheap for 4 days) and Mr. Trattle's fee was £5 5s. 0d.

To go to Portsmouth it was much quicker to go by sea as one could get there on the rising tide in a few hours at a cost of 5/–.

Sixty years afterwards in 1830 my great grandfather went to London for the first time and travel had by then so much improved that the journey took eleven hours but it was a terrible ordeal on the night coach, with the unmade roads: some travellers were very ill, in consequence.

---

1 Now fourteen.

Plan of Lymington c.1680:
1. Market Cross.
2. Shop Booths.
3. Old Town Hall.
4. Blind House.
5. The Abbot's Tenure.
6. Upper Well.

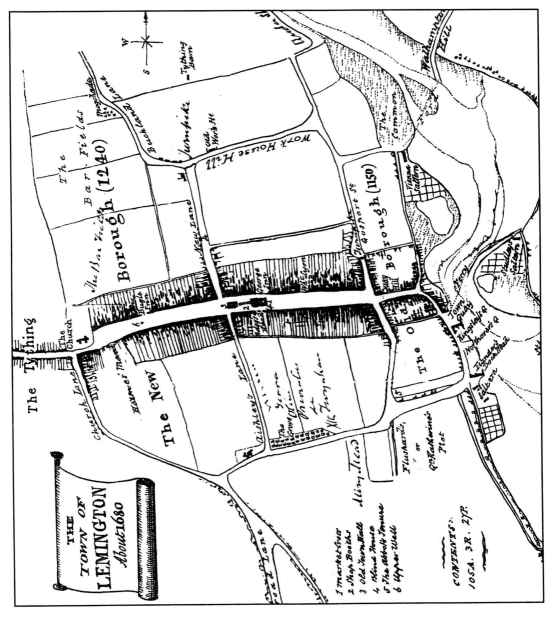

I have had the honour of naming two roads in recent years, Lyttletane Road after the first known Mayor of Lymington and Bingham Drive after Captain Bingham, later Admiral, who lived at The Grove, Church Lane.

The following roads I have never been able to trace, Spirit Lane, Green Lane, Clarks Lane, Parrotts Lane. The greatest crime is, I think, to change the name of an old house, this has been done in the case of Chantry Mead at Buckland which was, for 200 years, called Buckland Cottage and was the home of Mrs. Southey. In future years no one will know where she lived.

Our Walk starts at Ampress on the Borough boundary. An Artesian Well was sunk here about 1908 and at a depth of about 100 feet they brought up three sharks teeth, so many thousands of years ago our climate was tropical.

Buckland Rings next door is of course our Roman Fort. It is said that in 1704, two cwt. of coins were found here in two urns.

I always think that the British Camp was at Ravenscourt[1] (at Mr. Howlett's) or, as we knew it in my youth, Buckland Copse. It would be here that the Saxon inhabitants would drive their cattle via lower Buckland in time of invasion from the sea. When we had our first policemen it was here that they had their police post. In my youth the two cottages were still standing on the site of Mr. Howlett's house. The toll gate crossed the road at *The Crown Inn*[2]. I am glad to say that the Tollkeepers house is still standing.

From the Church Registers—1795 James Studley died; 77 years a Salt Boiler—kept the Gate. 1801 John Pocock—gatekeeper.

In the Church account an item appears yearly for 1/6½d., this was a tax of ¼d on every house and as this sum never varied it is quite probable that it dates from Saxon times, which will give us seventy four houses on and around the Quay. The Tax was known variously as Penticostals, Whitsun Farthings, Peter's Pence or Smoke Farthings and was paid to Winchester.

Our Borough received its charter in 1150 from Baldwin, Earl of Devon, being one of the very few Boroughs in England to receive its charter direct from the feudal lord. We received our freedom as we were on the extreme eastern end of the lords estate that stretched from Cornwall and also on the understanding that we would defend the town without help from outside.

Our town was burnt three times, 1338, 1370 and 1545. All the best buildings we have today date between 1700 and 1800.

Our roads until 1755, were appallingly bad—pigs routed in the gutters and had a yoke round their necks so that they could not invade the houses. Repairs were executed by ploughing and then faggots were laid in the deepest ruts and ploughed over. The first recorded expenditure in the Church books is in 1685, £2 10s. 4d. for the repairs of the towns roads.

The Turnpike act was passed in 1755 and from then on there was a great improvement. Turnpike gates were set up at each end of the town and money collected.

1784 Wilson Bays two days work pitching a way across the road opposite *The Angel* Inn 4/– labour 2/8, 69 ft. of pitchers at 4d per foot £1 3s. 0d. Total £1 9s. 8d. Two wheelbarrows and three pick axes £1 11s. 0d. 204 loads of gravel at 4d. per load £3 8s. 0d.

---

1   Since demolished and now Saxon Place.
2   Now *The Tollhouse Inn*.

These "ways" were stone sets laid across the street to allow people to cross the road but with the yearly addition of more gravel, the road on either side of the "way" was much higher and I well remember driving in a carriage up the street and the dreadful shock received when passing these dips. Crossing sweepers were employed at each "way" to keep them cleared and passengers gave coppers for this service. I only remember four of these crossings; at the Church, at *The Bugle*[1], *The Angel* and the corner of Gosport Street.

Let us now proceed with our walk. At *The Crown* inn there is a tunnel under the road. The entrance, now bricked up, is in the garden of the house opposite. This was probably made for the convenience of smugglers.

We next come to Buckland Cottage behind its high Wall—now renamed Chantry Mead— this was the home of Captain Charles Bowles of the East India Company who died in 1801 aged 63.

His daughter Caroline was born 1787—her mother was Ann Burrard—daughter of General G. Burrard commander in the Peninsular after Wellington. Her grandmother lived with them—always wore a black dress with lace cap and ruffles and a muslin apron. Hair powdered and turned back over a cushion. She was carried to Church in a Sedan chair. Caroline was passionately fond of animals. She had dogs, cats, rabbits, birds, dormice and a parrot. She married Southey the poet in 1839 at Boldre Church. Southey died in 1843 and Caroline died ten years afterwards in 1853.

Next-door to Buckland Cottage stands the charming 16th century Old Manor House. The room above the front door was always occupied by the master of the house and here he kept his musket and fishing rods. From here to *The Hearts of Oak*[2] were the extensive Barfields or Borough Fields going through to Lower Buckland: the inhabitants of the town drew lots every year for their strips of land and here they grew their corn and other crops, in the autumn it was thrown open for grazing by horses and cattle.

The Hearts of Oak, a very old inn, was formerly called *The Blacksmiths* and here stood one of the Town wells and a set of stocks.

Priestlands Place, otherwise Soapy Lane had a gate across the entrance known locally as Temple Bar and still commemorated by Temple Bar Cottage on the left. *The Waterloo Arms* stood in the vacant lot to the right. It was formerly called *The Bricklayers*.

Moving down the street we come to *The King's Arms* 1676 but rebuilt in 1935.

Phyllida[3], the dress shop across the street, is probably one of the oldest shops in this part of the town, dating from 1620. Across the road is Quadrille Court, named not after the dance but a card game played by the French Officers who met here during the French Revolution: an account of the game is given in Parson Woodford's diary. Many of the French refugees stayed on in Lymington long after the Revolution had ended. A Madelle Pailet was a tenant of my great grandfather for thirty years at a rent of £1. 1s. 0d. per week.

The Dorset Arms was formerly *The Fighting Cocks*[4]–owing to its bad reputation it was closed by Col. Hammersley, a magistrate, in 1882 and only allowed to reopen if the name was changed, hence the unimaginative *Dorset Arms. The Six Bells*[5] was an inn next door (at present

---

1   *The Bugle*. Now a branch office of a building society; 82 High St.
2   Now Hearts of Oak Cottage.
3   40 St Thomas' Street.
4   Now *The Fighting Cocks* again.
5   46, St Thomas' Street.

a shop) and named of course after the six bells in the Church Tower. It was the headquarters of the bellringers.

Just above this was Woodmancote, now pulled down, the home of Sir Giles Rooke Q.C. who died in 1808 aged 66, he was an ancestor of the Rookes of Woodside. Belmore Lane, formerly known as Townsend Lane, was all thatch but was burnt down in 1912. *The Millrights Arms* stood at the end and was closed in 1915. Further down the lane is Fairfield, the home of Ralph Allen Daniell since 1825. He had eight children:- Ralph, Capt. 84 regt., Edmund, Henry, Juliana, Laura (married Admiral Castle of New Lodge), Fanny (married Capt. Towsey R.N.), Adelaide (married Canon Maturin, a widower) and Robert Henry who lived afterwards at 3 Highfield. His four children were Reginald, Allen, Eve and Nora who married the late Dr. Maturin.

Afterwards Fairfield[1] had a tragic history—it was bought by a Captain Bouchier, but his bride died before the wedding. He kept the home, with all the furniture, empty for many years looked after by a housekeeper (Miss Knight).

Opposite the Church is Monmouth House, a house of great architectural interest:—two inch brickwork, thick window bars and a stone doorway of great interest—built about 1650 it was the home of Mrs. Knapton during the Rebellion of 1615. One night the Monmouth supporters met at the house but the King's men forced their way in during the meeting, whereupon the conspiritors escaped through the rear windows. Mrs. Knapton with great presence of mind wrapped a piece of flannel round her head and picking up one of the discarded clay pipes, puffed furiously, telling the troopers that it was the only way to cure her toothache. Afterwards the Rev. Ellis Jones lived here at the Vicarage. The town was so divided in its loyalties during this time that Thomas Dore the Mayor, raised a troop of horse and went off to fight for Monmouth. When all was over he received a free pardon.

Southend house in Church Lane has good doors and windows. I particularly like the curious lancet windows on the west side. Church Lane house is 1700c–1720c.

Elm Grove House[2] (about 1750) is of good design with stone window frames and an elegant curved garden wall. It is not well known that there are several walls like this (but not so good) behind the shops in the town, they are reputed to have been introduced by the French during the revolution.

Pilgrim[3] (Mr. Pitt) is a very good example of a gentleman's house of the period, possibly 1660. It has a beautiful garden—one of the best in Lymington.

The group of three Regency houses next to the church have some very fine doorways and fanlights. The first house was Murdoch's boys school. At Rashley's there was a nice pannelled room with a well designed corner niche. *The Bugle* inn is a derivation of Bubale, a wild ox: the sign was a bulls head with large horns. In 1675 they paid a yearly tax of 4d. for the sign. Parish Meetings were held here in the eighteenth century when a Mrs. Robinson was the landlady.

The Red House, about 1722, has been sadly altered, it had a fine circular hood to the door. It has some good panelling. Richard Sharp the solicitor lived here in 1900. Grosvenor House

---

1 Now demolished.
2 36, Church Lane.
3 58, High St. Opposite the Church; the garden is now largely housing.

was built in 1831 by James Munro who died in 1849 aged 75. His wife was Maria, daughter of Captain Samber R.N. It was also the home successively of The Rev. Bull and W. Robinson Hill, our well loved doctor.

Bellevue House[1] 1775 was the home of Mr. Hackman. It is a splendid example of a Georgian house—it is a building of excellent proportions with a magnificent stairway in oak, probably the best in Lymington. The two pavilions on either side are reputed to be converted from old cottages. At one time it was a very high class girls boarding school run by the Misses Noakes and Banks.

No.38, National Westminster Bank, has some very excellent oak pannelling and a curious stone door.

The Congregational Church was formed in Lymington in 1700. A Trust Deed of 1719 states that "a tenement the property of Ann Bulkly living in Old Lymington was then used as a Meeting house" (now Health Foods, St. Thomas Street).

Rev. James Pearson was the first Minister—from 1726–1796. The Church was called Presbyterian but later named Independent. In 1810 when the Rev. John Davies left after five years ministry there was no settled pastor for eleven years the services being taken by about seventy ministers from Dr. Bogue's Academy at Gosport. Then in 1820 a very remarkable man appeared, Rev. David Everard-Ford. He had been invited to take the office for a short period but when he found that there was a large debt of £1,150 still owing for alterations to the Chapel he had made up his mind to decline to stay.

Owing to the liberality of one of two wealthier members of the congregation the debt was soon paid off and Ford decided to stay. He stayed for twenty years. Ordination took place on September 21st 1825, starting at 10.30 and occupied nearly five hours. He was a composer of Church Music and wrote no fewer than seven music books (I have a copy) as well as six books on behalf of the Home Missionary Society.

He married a Miss Down, a school teacher of Plymouth and she opened a ladys' boarding school here which was very successful. To this school went my great grandfather's daughter. He was a close friend of my great grandfather who taught him the art of printing.

From here he had a call to Salford, Manchester a great advancement for him. He died on October 24th, 1875 while my great grandfather was on his death bed and was not told of the passing of his old friend.

The following is a good story of David Ford. In his musical days he had set an Anthem which was to be sung at one of the services and in which came the words "Hark the Trumpet". Unknown to the congregation he had secreted old Macey the town trumpeter under the pulpit and when the words "hark the trumpet" came, Macey blew a loud blast that startled the older members terribly. Afterwards the deacons hinted very plainly that, however artistic, this had better not be repeated.

The present Congregational Church[2] was proposed on July 13, 1843 and in two and a half years £2,000 was collected. Building commenced in 1847 and was completed in October the

---

1   48, High St. Now a solicitor's office.
2   Now the United Reformed Church.

Houses which once stood on the site of the present United Reformed Church. These were demolished prior to 1847 when the Congregational Church was built – it was this building that later became the United Reformed Church.

The Wheatsheaf Inn at the end of Gosport Street (*c*.1690). On the right is the old Isle of Wight Hoy named after the flat-bottomed vessels which conveyed man and beast to and from the island.

same year. The Church including the School and Parsonage cost £4,500 and the debt on opening day was only £300. One old lady travelled all over the neighbourhood collecting pennies and in five years collected £99.10s.

The last service in the Old Town Chapel was held on October 24th 1847.

On the site of the present chapel was the small house of Thomas Thirle, one of the last surgeon-barbers who used to do all the bleeding in the town. He was sixty six when he died in 1791.

On the site next door, now occupied by Elliotts[1] was Baileys China Shop, a greengrocers, and a gunsmith. On the corner of Ashley Lane in 1650 was Ashley (hence Ashley Lane) who made the bell ropes for the Church and the harnesses for bull baiting which took place behind in the present Grove Gardens. A very cruel sport but well patronised by the local inhabitants. Klitz's Music Shop[2] was *The Red Lion* inn in 1675.

So much is my interest in the people that I have now started buying the census forms from the Record Office—1841, 1851 and 1861, and in two months' time I shall have 1871. They are of enormous interest to me—all the people who I know so well by name I now know their ages, what the relationships are and even the maids in the houses. One curious thing about the 1841 census: the Government today asks you for an enormous amount of information but at that time all they wanted to know was your name and the people living in the house and they said you could put down any age within five years of your actual age! When you get to 1861 you get the correct age.

The biggest building in New Street is the Baptist Church; the Baptist community started in Lymington in 1688 with a small house in Captains Row. In 1769 they came to the present site, but the first church did not last long. The ground was given by a Mr. Lillington—the house next door to the church is Lillington House, evidently where he lived. In 1834 the original building was pulled down and the present one erected. Using the old materials, the building cost £1,625, legacies amounted to £1,275 leaving only £350 to be raised. It is interesting to note the pillars on the front of the church are similar to those of Grosvenor House, built in 1831, so it looks as if they were designed by the same architect.

The building next to the Baptist Church is the Literary Institute, which was the Lymington theatre, started in 1771. It must have been a very rickety building. A London company of James Stratford came for the summer months, there being no street lighting in the winter. In the Church Parish Register of 1800 is recorded the death of William Farren, aged 41, of Stratford's Company of Comedians. In 1847 the Literary Institute was built. A little passage next door led to the *Three Horseshoes* inn opened in 1775 and closed in 1878 by a magistrate for harbouring a policeman at night.

Eagle House and Hawthorn House were all one. Bowling Green House—a school run by a Dr. Davidson. In 1801 according to the census they had about thirty six boys there. It was a good school and boys came from all over the country.

The Community Centre was one of the barracks for the French Royalists who came over during the French Revolution; and after the disaster of the battle of Quiberon Bay when so many of the French were killed or captured, came the riff-raff of Europe and it became the

---

1   44, High St.
2   88, High St. Now a shoe shop.

quarters of the Dutch artillery company. Possibly, that is how we get the name Cannon Street. On the other side were open fields up to New Lodge, and there Spurgeon, the great non-conformist preacher in the 1880's, came to preach in a big marquee erected there. Next comes New Lodge, built in 1840 by Rear Admiral William Langford Castle. In 1862 he became a widower and married Laura, daughter of Ralph Daniel who lived at Fairfield—he died in 1874 aged 74 years.

Next door is the Poorhouse (now the Infirmary) which cost £4,500 to build. Then comes *The Borough Arms*, originally called *The Clippers Arms* (a clipper was a light chaise with two horses). When horses went out, it became *The Borough Arms* and has always been in the Joliffe family.

Back to the High Street, where we are able to see the Monument[1] which was put up to Sir Harry Burrard Neale. It cost £1,482.3s.

Lymington has had three poets. Coventry Patmore was born 1823 and died 1896. One of his most well known poems is "The Angel in the House". He was rather eccentric and came into town dressed in his dressing-gown—people in those Victorian days thought this was quite shocking. William Allingham lived in lodgings in Prospect Place (Ashley Lane)—a very lonely man who came here as a Customs Officer. From his life story he was not very happy because Victorian society would not accept him. He ingratiated himself with Tennyson in the Isle of Wight, and was always running over there. The Customs House was on the quay and whenever Tennyson came over, Allingham would see him on deck from his window and rush down to the station to welcome him and put him on the train.

The other local poet was Paul Verlaine, who was a French master at Murdoch's school next door to the church, where the Solicitors is now. He was a very weird man, born 1844, died 1896.

The next building, which is now SCATS[2], was built about 1840 as four flats, but for a considerable time it stayed empty so the local wags called it "Gibraltar"–"it was never taken"!

Langham Browne's[3] was originally St. Barbes' bank, 1786. I have my great grandfather's bank book–most of it appears to be speculating in property. St. Barbes' sign was a chequers sign, the oldest sign in the world as one was unearthed at Pompeii: it means anywhere that money is changed. Hence *The Chequers Inn* at Woodside was the Customs Office for the salt or Exchequer Office. After St. Barbe's death in 1826 at the age of 76 No. 91 became Corbins the chemist and 92 became Royle the solicitor. He was one of the solicitors for the Burrards when they put up for Parliament.

Moore and Blatch's office (Bellevue House)–one of the beauties of the house is it is all built of what is known in the building trade as "enders", that is bricks which are laid in endways–the walls are 18 inches thick so the windows are set back further than usual.

The first town hall was at Humphries[4] and the Bristol and West Office[5], set on pillars in the road and archways under which they kept the armoury for the town. It was given by Juliana Tevant who lived in Devonshire in 1467. The second one was opposite Langham Browne's built in 1684 and cost £220, afterwards becoming Fulford's School. It became a bit old fashioned as the Burrard family wanted to get their wealthy friends from London as burgesses

1 Across the river at Walhampton.
2 41-42, High St. Now a shoe shop.
3 91-92, High St. Now a newsagent.
4 31, High St. Now a ladies clothes shop.
5 30, High St. Now at 98, High St.

and wanted something better. They built a third town hall opposite Kings. About ten years ago the road was dug up there and while they had the road up I suggested they mark with studs in the road where the foundations were, but this was never done. The town well was immediately in front of *The Londesborough*[1] hotel entrance. The fourth town hall was in Earley Court, given by Miss Earley, and then the fifth one you know in Avenue Road. Presumably there must have been one before the Juliana Tevant, possibly on the Quay.

The house[2] on the corner of the bus station is about 1580, half timbered, with a venetian window in front, two square windows at the side and a nice circular one in the middle. *The Anchor and Hope*[3] was previously called *The Crown* (1747) and was burnt down in 1905. I well remember being pulled out of bed in the middle of the night–they thought the whole town was going to burn. It was a very old timbered building. The Telegraph Coach used to go from there at 5 a.m. You could only go to London either at 5 a.m. or 5.45 in the afternoon. It took 2½ hours to Southampton and 11 hours to London.

Long's Wine[4] shop was a gunsmith's–they used to have a lean-to over the shop front; old Mr. Finucane was the gunsmith. The National Provincial Bank[5] was originally a gentleman's residence and was Moore and Blatch's office till a few years ago, there is some nice panelling inside. The Midland Bank has a nice canopy on the first floor–it was Hayward's the butchers shop from 1832-1900. *The Nag's Head* was changed to *The Londesborough* because Lord Londesborough who was staying at Lyndhurst used to come into Lymington for his "eleven-ses". The landlord was so thrilled to be patronised by a real live lord that they tore down the old sign and made it *The Londesborough Hotel*.

I well remember an old man from Pennington who came into town for his wife's shopping. He came along the right hand side visiting every public house and came back on the left hand side doing the same—he was timed one day going into *The King's Arms* and it was something under 30 seconds as they had his drink all ready for him.

Shaw's Court, next to Humphries, was like every other court with lots of little houses. Shaw kept the shop where the jewellers[6] are now.

The Market Cross stood near the Town Hall and was pulled down in 1820, then came the whipping post and the stocks, the well and then the shambles (stalls on which butchers exposed their meat for sale) went up as far as New Street. The killing of cattle in the street was prohibited in 1745.

The Angel was originally *The George*, one of the oldest inns in Lymington — the earliest date known is 1675. It was before George I's time so was possibly named after St. George, the patron saint. There is a passage under the road from *The Angel* to *The Londesborough* possibly an old smugglers passage. Above the old coach house at the back, the one until recently occupied by the travel agent, there is a stone inscribed JH 1773. I saw a painter at work there one day and got him to paint it in in black. JH stands for John Hannaford who was the landlord when Rowlandson came down to Lymington, after the "Royal George" sank off Portsmouth. There is a picture of him with the landlady of *The Angel* — he calls her a pretty widow, and this turns out to be Mrs. Hannaford. There is a picture of the salt works

1   34, High St. Now a wine & spirit merchant and an optician.
2   Now demolished.
3   96, High St. Now a building society.
4   99, High St.
5   38, High St. Now National Westminster Bank.
6   33, High St.

and another of him going off in a chaise from *The Angel*. The coach that left there at 5.30 p.m. got to London about 4 o'clock in the morning.

A year or two ago they pulled down a chimney at *The Angel* and a child's shoe fell out. It was sent to the Boot and Shoe Manufacturers' Association at Nottingham and they said it was placed in the chimney to bring fertility to the house—it might be 200 years old.

Kings was a Private Bank and wine merchants run by Mr. West—underneath are the remains of the old wine bins. 106 was a chemist's shop entered by a side door. If you look on the ceiling on the right hand side there is a painted sign advertising chemist's goods.

The Assembly Rooms were built in 1805, possibly by French labour. Navarino Court was named after the battle in 1827 when the British, French and Russian fleets under Admiral Codrington defeated the Turks off the coast of Greece. Similarly, you will find Nelson Place, Trafalgar House, etc. Where the Abbeyfield shop[1] is now, there are some bricked up windows–this was to avoid the window tax of 1697, which cost something like 4d. a window–this tax was abolished in 1851. In the parish books you will find in 1769 the death of Stephen Kneller, a surveyor of windows.

Humphries and Bristol and West have very nice bow windows on the first floor. Hapgoods[2], Myles Cooper[3], *The Red Lion* and the cake shop[4] are a quartet with splendid bay windows. *The Red Lion* dates from around the 1600's and if you go into the back room you will see some old bottle glass with the name of one of the landlords, William Virling, dated 1803. *The Albion* stood a bit back from the road on the sight of the present Masonic Hall. It was pulled down and remained empty ground for many years.

Stanwell House, where I went to school, was originally a gentleman's residence, earlier, the second offices of Moore and Blatch's. The Roman Catholic priest's house is a very nice building dating back to about 1720. It was the home of the Oviat family who had fishing fleets in Newfoundland and they used to send over from Lymington fish hooks and salt, and then bring back wine from the Mediterranean to Lymington. Samuel Oviat died in 1791.

Balls old shop No. 2 and 3 is probably the oldest shop in Lymington—possibly built before 1620 because of the overhanging roof boards in front. Gutters were brought in from the Dutch about 1620. No. 1 High Street is peculiar because they have got three bays over each other. It was the home of the well known Hicks family in 1830.

The Grove in Grove Road dates from 1690, the same period they put in lime trees in the churchyard. Two years ago the Corporation cut the tops off these trees, and so our Grove that had lasted 280 years was killed at a stroke.

The first post office was Galpine's, Klitz's shop, and the second was at Corrall's shop[5]. The third was at Smith's the chemists and the fourth where the Ministry of Pension are and the fifth where Home Mead was (the present site).

On Quay Hill–Nos. 7 and 4 have nice doorways, and there is a circular window on No. 11. *The Solent Inn*[6] down the hill must have been a gentleman's residence. It has a gigantic chimney on the north side, and curiously enough it has a lovely knocker on the front door, a lion's head, the same as Moore and Blatch's. Mr. Yateman used to keep it when it was a public

---

1   On the site of the new Barclay's Bank.
2   112, High St.
3   114, High St.
4   115, High St.
5   84, High St.
6   Now Old Solent House.

house. He weighed about 23 stone; once going to a football match at Brockenhurst by train, I saw some men put him on the station scales.

Flushards is "Fleshettes" (the flesh fields), and there they used to kill the cattle. A few years ago a workman said "come and see what we have found". Digging a ditch to put in a cable at Cory's yard[1], they had found dozens of cattle horns in a very dirty condition. It was interesting because when they killed the cattle they used to take the horns down to the river and throw them in. They must be about 400 years old.

When they had slain the cattle, the oxheads were sold to the poorhouse. It is supposed to be a very nice part of the animal, and in an old book I found how to make oxhead soup. It said–take half an oxhead 10d., 1 lb. barley 3d., 6 lbs. potatoes 3d., pepper and salt 1d. onions 1d. a lb, carrot and turnips 2d, water 22 pints, total 1/8d. It makes three gallons–enough for eight men for the most laborious work for dinner and supper. They fed them on oxheads, beef at 6d a lb, and veal at 4d, and they drank lees, the dregs from beer barrels, mixed with water.

Gosport Street ended at *The Wheatsheaf*[2] (note the ironwork on the sign) where there was another stocks, and a third one was in Southampton Road. In that piece of ground where Trafalgar House is built, was *The Isle of Wight Hoy*, a very old inn. It was so called because the hoys used to travel to the Isle of Wight from near this point—a flat bottomed boat which took cattle and people from the quay once every day there and back. Probably the call "ship ahoy" comes from this source.

The old police station, now Queen Anne's Restaurant[3], was the home of Dr. Towsey's family: the first man my great-grandfather met when he came here to join his uncle in his business. He walked from Yeovil in two days. Dr. Towsey's burial place is just outside the vestry door with iron railings around it—the only one which did not have them taken away during the War. On the corner was *The Plume of Feathers* (the Prince of Wales' Feathers) and opposite was *The Star* inn, a little house with blue and red bricks alternately. When they built the railway station in 1858 a lot of these houses with blue and red bricks were built there—these bricks were only in vogue for a short period. On a visit to the Burley Manor Hotel where similar bricks have been used, I enquired when it was built. This was built about 1852, so I was able to date the houses in Station Street. The Methodist Church was built on its present site because it was thought that with the coming of the railway station this part of the town was going to expand, but this did not happen. The station was originally a hut just inside the gates going over the bridge. Underneath that hut was the first station bell, which I have in my keeping. The Town Mill (tidal) stood behind the present bus building in Station Yard—the station yard was the millpond—John Dexter was the last known miller.

The bridge was built in 1735—originally it was a solid bridge with no gates, and when you went over the other side there was an open bridge and the tide used to come up that side. It was built by Captain Cross, a descendant of a favourite of Charles II, who gave to Captain Cross's ancestor all the mudlands between Calshot and Hurst Castle, and he built this bridge to make a little money. The river used to be much wider and deeper and they used to lay up

---

1   Now the car park on the Quay.
2   Now Wheat Sheaf House.
3   Now Peelers Bistro.

The Solent Inn, Quay Hill. Built originally as a gentleman's residence in about 1700. This early photograph of William Stephen's brewery and public house can be compared to a later view showing how the ground floor was converted in the last years of the 19th century.

the salt ships there for the winter months, in tiers three or four abreast. Mrs. Rachael Cross, his widow, died in 1752.

In 1693 a house in Nelson Place cost £27; in 1697 it sold for £50; 1775 for £75; and possibly today it is worth more than £6,000[1].

Moore and Blatch was started by John King who lived at the Brackens, Captains Row. It became King and Moore, and had many changes of name until its present title.

In Captains Row was a girls school run by a Mrs. Young in 1803. An advertisement found for the school showed:—four–six years 6/– per quarter; six–nine years 8/– per quarter; nine years 9/– per quarter; plus writing extra 7/–; embroidery and print work included for 9/–. A footnote states "strictest attention is paid to their morals".

Bath Road was only built in 1832, before that the water came up to the bank where the council houses are now. Queen Katherine Road is named after Katherine Parr, wife of Henry VIII (the Flushards being her dowry).

---

1   1972 valuation. (Today houses here fetch £150,000 or more.)
2   16, High St.
3   Now Preacher's Bistro.

Over the period of the years, several cannon balls have been dug up dating from the last invasion in 1545–they weigh about 15-16lbs. When Mr. Elgar was building a house behind his shop[2] one of these was dug up. This is the farthest up the street one has ever been found.

The last house on the right hand side in Bath Road is *The Harlequin* inn—the old head-quarters of the Pressgang. They used to drink there and when a ship hove into sight they would go down and take off the men they wanted. Opposite was Legge's Baths—rather a disreputable place.

Thomas Inman owned the boatyard (where the Berthon boatyard is now). He was born at Hastings and about 1816 he got into a boat with his family and belongings and came to Lymington to take over the shipyard. South Hayes was built by Edwin, son of Thomas—the wall around it cost £5,000 to build. The Old Drill Hall was built by Thomas Inman as a sail loft.

Beeston's Baths (the present swimming baths) advertised a warm bath for 3/6, shower 2/6, a cold bath with a guide 1/–, without a guide 6d. The guide was the man who held you up by a rope.

Jack-in-the-Basket: the fishermen from Lymington used to go out in the Solent and to save them time their wives rowed down the river in punts and tied their food and drink in a basket on the last stake in the river. The drink was carried in "black jacks" (a tarred leather flask), hence Jack-in-the-Basket.

In 1750 rates were about 4d. in the £1. When the poor rate officers ran out of money they made up another rate. They kept strict observations of what they spent on the poorhouse. It cost 1/3d to keep a man in the poorhouse for a week, but they were well fed. The highest rated house in the town was rated at £40, next £30 and so on to the lowest at under £3.

The house in Ashley Lane, now "Foresters"[3] was a children's school. Looking through the deeds, it used to be called Almond's Lane, and above that used to be cottages.

Fairfield House was built about 1770—I have a picture showing an archery party on the lawn.

Waterford Lane is probably so called because it used to be under water before they built the banks in 1832.

"The Tins", the passage from the churchyard to Southampton Road, used to be lined with corrugated iron, hence its name.

In the course of time even the names of the roads have altered. I will record them here:-

Old Town—St. Thomas Street	Amen Corner—the bottom of Cannon Street
Old Town Lane—Queen Street	Pipemakers—top end of Buckland
Townsend Lane—Belmore Road	Mirey Mead—at Diamond's Workshop
Leybridge—Belmore Lane	Croydon—Lower Buckland
Orchard Close—West Hayes	Botany Bay—Mill Lane
Leg of Mutton Field—where Church Lane and Waterford Lane divide	Temple Bar—the top end of St. Thomas Street. A gate was across the road here.
Chatham Place—the end of Madeira Walk in Captains Row	Shaws Court—next to Humphries
Hunter's Piece—The Timber Yard in Captains Row	Victoria Court—halfway down hill, left hand side.
	Union Hill—now East Hill.

The 1801 and 1811 census is in four little books—North Lymington, South Lymington, Woodside and Buckland. It tells you who the people are etc.

The High Street in 1898. The clock shows us it is 10 o'clock and the shops appear to be open so we must assume it is not a Sunday. Despite this there are only five vehicles to be seen and one of these is a hand cart.

A 'busy scene' in St Thomas' Street at around the turn of the century. The lone pedestrian would not feel too out of place if he found himself in the same spot today.

Parliamentary Representation

From 1584, under a Charter granted by Queen Elizabeth, Lymington was granted the right to send two members to Parliament. In the seventeenth century Lymington was a typical Pocket Borough, the Members of Parliament being returned by a handful of Burgesses, and was controlled by the Burrard family. In the last election before the Reform Bill of 1832, 17 electors returned two Members. In 1832 the Parliamentary Borough was extended and the electorate enlarged, but even then there were only 243 electors to return two M.Ps. In 1867 the Membership was reduced to one. By the Re-distribution of Seats Act, 1885 Lymington became merged in the New Forest Division of the County of Southampton. In 1918 Lymington was included in the New Forest and Christchurch Division, but in 1948 the New Forest constituency was restored.

A PARLIAMENTARY ELECTION OF 1832

Lymington until the Reform Bill of 1832 was always a close borough and until 1868 sent two members to Parliament. Its representation had been regulated in the reign of Queen Elizabeth in the year 1585 but until that year it was often troublesome and maybe dangerous to be a member of parliament in the sixteenth century. The journey alone from Lymington to London was not one to be undertaken lightly. The roads—mere cart tracks by todays standard made travelling both tedious and dangerous, even a journey on horseback to the county town of Winchester, thirty miles, occupied two days. But with the accession of William and Mary all this changed, lucrative offices and high official positions were to be obtained by those who supported the party in Parliament so that elections were now closely and fiercely contested.

The election of 1832 is of particular interest as the expenses of this election have been preserved and they give a very clear picture of how our forebears conducted themselves on these occasions.

The election took place in July 1832 the contestants being Sir Harry Burrard Neale, Bart. and John Stewart in the Tory interest and Captain John Blackiston for the Whigs.

THE ACCOUNTS

1832 Election Expenses: Sir Harry Neale, Bart. (July 3–14, 1832).

	£	s	d
(*The Wheatsheaf*) James Smith 56½ Gallons of beer at 2/– gal.	5	13	0
(*The Fighting Cocks*) Wm. A. Green, 55 gallons best beer at 2/– gal.	5	10	0
(*The Angel*) Wm. Hebberd 56½ gallons beer at 2/– gal.	5	13	0
(*The Dolphin*) Lane Brett 112 Tickets for beer	5	12	0
	£22	**8**	**0**

R. Galpine A/c. for Printing:—

Tickets: 112 (*The Fighting Cocks*)		4	6
„ 112 (*The Brewery*)		4	6
„ 112 (*The Wheatsheaf*)		4	6
„ 112 (*The Dolphin*)		4	6

448

N.B. Tickets Value ½ Gal each = 224 Gallons.

Paid Ringers of Lymington Band by order of your Committee for ringing and during your Canvas	4	4	0
Paid Mr. Green (*The Fighting Cocks*) for refreshments for Ringers ordered by your Committee	1	1	0
Paid for Overseers Lists of Voters		16	0
Paid Mr. Wm. Good for silk flag etc.	4	19	2
Paid Wm. Knight for Flag Hire during the Canvas and Election	3	11	6
Paid Wm. Ackland do. do.	2	19	0
Paid Drivers including John Dyer paid by order of the Committee		19	0
Paid Mr. Sexton for use of Rooms at *The Angel* and for refreshments for your Committee during the Canvas	14	5	1
Paid Mr. Fowler for expenses incurred for refreshments during the revising Barristers sitting	3	5	0
Paid Mr. Wm. Grinsell a bill for Tolls paid at Lymington Bridge on the day of nomination etc.	1	17	1
Paid Mr. W. Hibberd for Beer given to man for fixing flagstaff and to the Band and money paid man for carrying flag on the Day of Nomination	1	4	0
John Blake a Bill for flag poles etc.	1	4	0
Mr. Hannolt for cash paid by him on several occasions during the Canvas and Election	2	1	6

Mr. Moore for cash paid by him during the Canvas at Boldre for refreshments etc.		12	0
Mr. Royle for hire of a Fly and for cash paid by him for copies of Lymington Poor Rates and Boldre Overseers Lists	1	6	9
Dinner for the Committee and friends at *The Angel* on the Day of nomination	36	11	7
Ditto on first day of Polling	45	5	0
Ditto on second day of Polling	27	15	0
Your Moiety of the general bills for Election dinners and for beer given to the Populace	250	0	0
Your Moiety of Mr. Figgs and Mr. Warne's bills for repairing windows belonging to *The Angel* and *The Nag's Head* inns and several private houses broken by the Mob on the Close of the Election	16	0	0
Your one-third part of the returning Officers expenses paid for the hire of rooms etc. on the days of nomination and election and which falls on the three Candidates	22	6	4
Your one Moiety of Extra Expenses paid by returning Officer and which falls on the two successful Candidates	12	12	7
Your one Moiety of the fee paid to the Under Sheriff on the notices of this Event, Stamps, Token Cards and Town Sergeants fees etc. etc.	22	14	1
Fee of Messrs. Rickman and Royle, Solicitors as your Agents during the whole	100	0	0
contest Ditto Messrs King and Moore, Solicitors	100	0	0
	677	9	8

Details:—

Colbornes Bill for Hustings	37	5	0
Fowler for Rooms	12	5	0
Polling Boards		6	0
Printing do.	1	0	0
Polling Booths		8	0
Deputees	8	8	0
Clerks	4	4	0
Ringers	3	3	0
	66	19	0
One third	22	6	4
Sheriff and Clerk	12	12	0
Messenger and Stamps	1	13	6
Stamps for Returns and Engrosing	4	3	2

Messenger Postage and Carriage	..	..	..	..	..	..	..				8	4
Galpines Bill	..	..	..	..	..	..	..	..	..	1	7	2
Town Clerk as usual	..	..	..	..	..	..	..	..	21	0	0
Sergeant	..	..	..	..	..	..	..	..	..	4	4	0
										45	8	2
Your half	..	..	..	..	..	..	..	..	..	22	14	1

It is nice to know that after this vast expense in dinners and beer Sir Harry Burrard was elected.

CHAPTER FOUR

Memorandum
Respecting the Trade of Lymington by W. Towsey

(Note Dr. Towsey lived in what was the old Police Station, Gosport Street).

It is to be inferred that a considerable trade to Newfoundland, Spain and Portugal was carried on from Lymington, during the 17th Century and beginning of 18th, from the tradition which exists, that a Tier of Vessels used to be laid up on the River, above the present bridge and causeway during winter, as well as from the circumstance that a family now in the town, is in possession of considerable property from their ancestors, who had acquired it as merchants and fish hook makers for that trade, likewise from the names of Wharfs and docks above the bridge which are found in old maps and writings. In Charles 1st reign, 1626, a considerable support was given to the salt trade (which must have existed in Lymington from a very remote period) by a grant of all the mudlands on the coast and this probably carried the capital which had been employed in other ways to be transfered to it.

In 1720 a trade in salt was carried on to Holland in Lymington Vessels and it was in one of these commanded by one of the family (John Northover) before attended to, that Peter the Great of Russia took his passage to England on which occasion Peter presented him with a silver cup. At length the Cheshire salt being produced from Pits and hives by a less expensive process than that made from sea water, was sold for less than the Lymington salt and consequently nearly drove the latter from the foreign market; still however the trade of the South coast of England aided by the medicinal salts which, at that time, were only made from sea water proved lucrative and a good accumulation of capital was made in it by many individuals until the close of the last war in 1815. Soon after that period the heavy duty on salt was taken off, and this operated to the disadvantage of the salt trade of Lymington, because the retailer on the south and west coasts were unable with a small capital to take in cargoes of Cheshire salt which they had not the means of doing whilst the heavy duties existed. During the last war, the depot for foreign troops was at Lymington and caused a considerable expenditure and circulation of money; many individuals in consequence accumulated capital, much of it still remains in the town. At present the principle dependence of the trades people is on the various independent gentlemen and families who live in the town and neighbourhood: and although this is very valuable to them, yet it cannot keep the town in that rank which its former additional sources of productive industry enabled it to hold. It is therefore highly desirable, that some means may be found for the productive employment of the industry and capital which exists in the town. The precident of a town of as near similar consequence as possible, Bridport in Dorset, having been granted the priviledge of a port a few months is in point. With the natural advantages of Lymington in point of situation as a port and with its excellent roadstead it cannot be doubted that were it opened as a Port the spirit and communual skill of the inhabitants would soon draw a trade to it. As the heavy entrances and tonnage duties are now much reduced in the French ports, a treaty with them would soon arrive: it is known that a vessel built in Lymington, has made the passage from Cherburg to within Jack in less than seven hours. The trade with the Western Islands for fruit is one which is likely to be entered into, as there is no place more proper for commencing the voyage, indeed a vessel built in Lymington and partly owned there, sailed during the present year in that trade. The ancient trade to the Newfoundland Fisheries and to Spain and Portugal might be renewed. The Oviatt family have, or of late years had, a station for fishing on the Newfoundland coast which their ancestors in Lymington used. The Pilot trade is one often productive of great profit and advantage to the Port from when it is carried on, ships in distress or derelect being often brought in; from which business occurs, Attorney's Ship-wrights, rope and sail makers and others; why should not Lymington partake of this.

There was a letter a few months since in the Newspapers addressed to masters of ships, stating that the writer had made many voyages as the master of a West Indiaman, that he had often been obliged to put back in at the Needles, the pilots always taking him to Cowes or the Motherbank, but on the last occasion, in the absence of a pilot he brought the ship in himself and came to an anchor in Lymington Road, where he found the best of holding ground and found also that he could get supplies at Lymington, with all necessary and comforts much cheaper and better than at the places he before was accustomed to; and added to this, he was much better placed for recommencing his voyage, and this he publishes for the benefit of his brother traders.

Were Lymington a port, the Pilot would more frequently land the passengers from the West Indiamen as being the nearest and most convenient place, they do so now occasionally, but the passengers are obliged to go on to Southampton to have their luggage cleared and those who have once felt the inconvenience of that, take care upon the next occasion, not to be landed at Lymington again, as happened only in the last week, when a party actually bound to Lymington chose to go on to Southampton.

The timber trade is one which would no doubt be entered into and many others would occur to the enterprising capatalists.

When at the close of the late war, the Govt. were understood to have wished to have thrown open every source of productive industry, the inhabitants of Lymington memorialised the Lord of the Treasury to open Lymington as a port, and their Lordships answer was that

The Quay c.1700. The house in the centre became the Customs House in 1850.

their Lordships had referred the memorial to the principal officers of the customs at Southampton who replied that there was not sufficient capital in Lymington to warrant such a step an assumption not true at the time and much less so now.

The answer from the Officers of the Customs at Southampton is just such a one as might have been expected from that quarter, but it is rather hard on the inhabitants of Lymington, that they should have been deprived of the opportunity of turning to account the natural advantages, and the capital which they undoubtedly possess, by any fiscal regulations.

The expense attendant on a port would probably be urged by Govt. as a reason for not opening Lymington, but there is no doubt that there are persons in Lymington, who could give ample security for the execution of the two superior officers, who would execute them gratuitously, until the trade of the Port should warrent the payment of the usual salaries.

(*from the Burrard Papers*).

Boiling pans at a Lymington salt works in 1787.

A boiling house possibly at the Pennington Marsh pans – with pumping windmills in the background.

CHAPTER   FIVE

The Manufacture of Salt

Salt from the earliest times has been the staple manufacture of Lymington and the salt-houses were a conspicuous feature of the coastline from Pylewell to Hurst.

It is only here and there that the embanked lands on which the salt pans were formed can now be traced and the salt houses have now all gone except possibly for one lone shed at Lower Woodside which may have been a storehouse only.

The Salt houses were of all sizes, some had only one boiling pan while others had twenty or more pans at work.

The Salterns proper were made on flat land divided into shallow pools about twenty feet square by low mudbanks a few inches high. Into these ponds the water was first scooped by large wooden balers from the ponds which had caught the water at high tides and here it was allowed to evaporate. Here and there throughout the works were small windmills about twelve feet high which continually pumped the water into different sets of pans until reaching the condition of brine it was lifted to large cisterns from whence it ran direct to the boiling houses.

These were large brick sheds with low walls with a wide expanse of tiled roof to within a few feet of the ground under which were the pans and furnaces. A cloud of steam filled the boiling house and salt impregnated the air while the roads around were black with ashes from the furnaces which had for generations been incessantly burning.

In 1743 there were 163 pans in operation from Pylewell to Hurst and I may here put on record some of the sites.

Vienna Saltern—Lymington Slipway	3 pans.
One off Town Quay—Lymington Laundry	12 ,,
One on site of Shipyard	5 ,,
One off Coastguard Station	3 ,,

The Old Manor House, Woodside.

Kings Saltern—Lymington Baths						22	pans
Oxey Saltern or Vineys						2	,,
Stone and Rowe—Woodside						20	,,
Troy Town (Oxey)						28	,,
Pennington Marsh						23	,,
Keyhaven						29	,,

Sixteen weeks boiling was the average for a season and each pan made three tons of salt per week, burning nineteen bushels of coal for each ton.

A drift or turn took eight hours after which the pan had to be cooled and cleaned.

Sixteen drifts made a weeks work which extended from Sunday night to Saturday morning. The actual value of the salt was 1/– per bushel but the Govt. duty was no less than 10/– per bushel.

Such a large industry needed a considerable number of inspectors and their office was at Lower Woodside Green, where riding officers, clerks and boatmen were stationed. These comfortable positions were considered a legitimate heritage for the free burgesses and their many relatives.

The end came in 1865 when owing to the introduction of Cheshire Salt it was no longer a paying proposition and the last salthouse "Rowes" was closed in that year.

The marshes were then more or less levelled and became useful for grazing grounds, the old boiling houses were removed so that today little trace can be seen of what once was of great commercial importance and had been going on here before historical times and to have had a reputation from the earliest periods of history.

CHAPTER SIX

The Poor House

From the early days of the history of England the monasteries had always been the main source for the relief of the poor–in fact everything we read of life in the Middle Ages brings to our minds a picture of the poor at the gate duly receiving bread, meat and a dole of money. This custom represented an ancient tradition of Christianity which was of the greatest value but in practice it was unorganised and indiscriminate and possibly did as much to increase the number of beggars as to reduce them.

At the dissolution of the monasteries in the reign of Henry VIII this source of relief came to an abrupt end and it was not long before "bands of sturdy beggars" began to terrorise the countryside and it became an urgent necessity for the government of the day to act.

Thus we see in the reign of Elizabeth I the beginnings of the Poor Law when it became the duty of every parish to provide for the poor within its boundaries by the levying of rates and the provision of materials to provide work for the able bodied, such as flax, hemp, wool and thread.

No doubt the system was imperfect and more so in some districts than others, but a national system existed both in theory and fact and the provision now provided for the poor was better than anything seen before and better than anything seen in Europe for many generations to come. In fact it can be said that the provision for the poor made in the reign of Elizabeth I, in no small measure saved our country from the horrors of revolution which swept France in the late 18th century.

Another aspect of the Poor Law was the question of removal—this enabled the Parish officers to send back to his place of birth any man, together with his family, who became chargeable to the rates—the fear this instilled in the minds of the authorities caused them to exercise their powers in some cases harshly and sometimes too at enormous expense— many cases of this will be noted here, for instance:—

Coachman to carry Richard Whitehead and family from Lymington to Huntingdon and Guardian from Huntingdon to Lymington £17 1s. 0d. Expenses of journey £1 12s. 10d., it should be noted that the Guardian always accompanied the family however long or short the journey.

In the first instance the relief of the poor was made the responsibility of the Church Wardens but they were already busy men with manifold duties to perform and as the problem grew beyond their power, new officers were created called the Overseers of the Poor.

These, two in number, were elected yearly in Easter Week at the same time as the appointment of the Church Wardens and they thereafter met once a month on Sunday after Divine Service. One of the many duties of these Overseers was the putting-out or apprenticing of children—boys from 7 to 24 years and girls from 7 to 21 years or marriage. A list of the principal Townspeople who were deemed suitable to take apprentices was kept in the back of the Minute Book, thus we see in 1783 the list comprised 64 names. The sum of £2 was allowed the person who took the child but should they refuse when called upon to do so they forfeited the sum of £10 for the use of the poor or in other words the relief of the rates.

Workhouses were established in the 9th year of the reign of George I that is in 1723 but it was not until 15 years afterwards in 1738 that the first Lymington house for the reception of the poor was built at a cost of £248 10s. 0d.

1st day of June 1738. It is ordered and agreed by us the Parish Officers—parishioners of Lymington aforesaid whose names are hereinunto subscribed—Messrs. Richard Chalk, Roger Beere and Obder Knapton and the Overseers of the Poor for the time being. Do as soon as convenient may be, enter into Articles of Agreement with William Beeston on behalf of the parish for building a Charity House adjoining to the Alms House according to the proposals and a plan delivered in and by them signed this day, and at and under such proper Covenants and agreements as the said Richard Chalk, Roger Beere and Odber Knapton and the Overseers of the Poor shall think fit—for the benefit and advantage of the parish and do and shall from time to time visit and inspect such building to see that the same be done in a good workmanlike way and manner and with good and sufficient materials and that if any defect shall arise concerning the same then the said Inspectors shall from time to time acquaint the parish therewith at a proper meeting or meetings to be called for that purpose.

Jno Burrard	Henry Holloway	William Mitchell Junr.
Roger Beere	Obad Newell	Jos Pearce
Jn Northover	Richard Curtis	Jno Bampton
John Oviatt	Saml Colborne	Thomas
Richard Chalk	Phillip Blake	Jas Burt
Joseph Sparrow	John Bay	Gregory Missen
Jacob Marks	Kneller	
Joseph Dike	Jno Barnford	
Robert Welsh	Tho Sparrow	

The position of this house can be seen on the plan some 90 yards down East Hill on the left hand side and the position of the gate is still discernable where the wall breaks away to form a narrow grass verge.

The Poor Books still in existence are as follows:—

1785 – 1791	1805 – 1811	1823 – 1829
1791 – 1799	1811 – 1815	1829 – 1832
1799 – 1805	1815 – 1818	1832 – 1835

Overseers Daily Books 4to.:— 15 in all
Overseers Monthly a/c Books Fscap.:
1774 – 1782; 1782 – 1787; 1787 – 1795; 1795 – 1800; 1800 – 1807.
Overseers Monthly a/c Books Fscap. cont'd.:—1807 – 1816; 1816 – 1827.
Minute Books:— 1775 – 1785; 1791– 1816.

Unfortunately the opening books of the first Overseers are not now in existence—as our first monthly a/c book begins in April 1774 that is 36 years after the opening of the Poor House and the first Minute Book starts on May 16, 1775.

The Monthly Account Books are long folio 16½ x 6½ inches and are copies written in the fair hand of the Vestry Clerk from the Overseers Daily Books. Each of the two Overseers appear to have kept his account monthly in turn and while the writing and spelling of the Account Books is very good indeed, that of the Overseers Daily Books is at times extremely poor and the spelling even more so. The following examples will show the difficulty experienced in reading these books.

Childring = children
Bisness = business
Carre = carry
Briches = breeches
Famle = family
Ounder shour = under shore

Tenden on ye Jostes = attending the Justices
Wief = wife
Goen to Plymouth = going to Plymouth
Backey and snouf = tobacco and snuff
Gounds = gowns
Pareaches Bisnes = Parish business

and the following sentences:
Paied Mary alcocsander for meaken a gound for rolens gual.
Man with a pass to Chatme
Droen a touth for Meare hart

Richard Budden was appointed the first Master in May 1739 at a salary of £10 and Henry Hackman was appointed "to provide the necessary medicines and proper assistance in surgery" at a salary of £10.

An Inventory of the Goods belonging to Lymington Workhouse, April the first 1741.

Long Table	1	Cotterl	1
Forms	4	Crane	1
Stool	1	Irons for Linen	2
Hourglass	1	Bellows	1 pair
Great Chairs	2	Pepper Box	1
Small Chairs	6	Trenchards	20
Grid Irons	2	Mugs	6
Large Grates	1 pair	Spade	1

Poker	1	Shuffing Iron	1
Firepan	1	Pillows	4
Tongs	2 pair	Rugs and Coverlets	12
Heater	1	Bolster Cloaths	
Table Cloaths	2	Skillet	1
Chest	1	Meashing Tub	1
Bucket	1	Stand	1
Sweeping Brush	1	Tubs	2
Hand Brush	1	Small covers	4
Rubbing Brush	1	Colder	1
Brush for Cloths	1	Salt Glass	1
Copor	1	Spoons	18
Cover	1	Close Stool	1
Grates	1 pair	Howe	1
Brass pott	1	Feather Beds	6
Iron potts	2	Chafe Beds	6
Saucepan	1	Blankets	18
Pillow	1	Large Frying Pan	1
Long Towels	2	Flesh forks	1 pair
Grain Tubs	2	Earthen, pots, pans and dishes	20
Renge	1	Wooden platters	2
Pail	1	Scimmer	1
Buckets	2	Ladle	1
Boldish	1	Wooden Dishes	2
Sieve	1	Knives	3
Powdering Tub	1	Wheelbarrow	1
Half hogs heads	4	Rake	1
Salt Tub	1	Feather Bolsters	6
Stands	2	Chaff Bolsters	6
Funnel	1	Sheets	14
Pillowcase	1	Hoggs Trows	2
Bedsteads	4		

1741, June 6th.

At a vestry this day held at the usual place in the Parish Church of Lymington. It is ordered that the Churchwardens and overseers of the poor of this parish do forthwith pay to Mr. William Samber the sum of £15 for the purchase of his house or cottage (with the appurtenances in this parish) called "The Doggs Kennell" and that the said churchwarden and overseers do take a grant and a conveyance of the said premises from the said Mr. Samber in their Names in Trust for the Parishioners of this parish for the time being. And it is further ordered that the overseers of the poor of this parish do forthwith Enlarge, Repair or otherwise Amend the said Premises or Lazaretto or Hospital fit, proper, and Convenient for the Reception and Entertainment of such Person or Persons as shall happen to be visited with the smallpox or other infectious Deseases within the said parish and in such Manner as they the said overseers shall think fit.

Mr. William Samber mentioned above lived at what is now the old Police Station in Gosport Street but the actual position of "The Doggs Kennell" is not known, we are inclined to think the most likely spot would be on a plot of land near the present railway line, about half way to Ampress.

1756, Smallpox, May 31st.

It was ordered and agreed by the Parishioners that the Churchwardens and Overseers of the Poor shall be indemnified of and from all costs and charges that shall or may happen on account of Edward Bradeing of West Cows, bringing to this place Jane Kent with the Smallpox then fresh out upon her.

From May 1768 to August 1769; 59 deaths.

From October 1778 to December 1779; 26 Deaths.

1757.

At a Vestry Meeting held 18th December 1757, it is ordered and agreed that ye Overseers of ye Poor shall purchase and lend to Susanna Colborne, widow, a furnace and also to give her a Brewing of Malt etc.

1760, April 8th.

That whereas William Collins the present Master has been paid 1/6d per week for some years past for each and every poor person victualised by him.

It is now ordered that for the time to come the Parish Officers do not pay unto the said William Collins more than 1/3d per week.

3rd June 1762.

It is hereby ordered that the Churchwardens and Overseers shall pay towards providing nine Substitutes and Volunteers which our Parish is now to provide the sum of £6 for each and every Substitute or Volunteer so by them provided.

Every parish was called upon to provide "volunteers" for the army.

1774.

The Overseers Account Books open in 1774, the Overseers being Hart and Rickman.

The first page lists the names of 31 persons receiving out door relief some of 1/– only, others at 1/6, then follows a list of occasional reliefs and such items as "to Thomas Elling a gallon Loaf 1/2.

"To Umphry Wright to go to Portsmouth"	3	0
"A pair of shoes for Whites' Child"	2	6
"Tobacco and Snuff"	4	0
"A poor Man"		6

The total of this account for one month is £16 1s. 11d. and is verified by the two Church-wardens, Sam Oviatt and W. Hayward followed by seven members of the Vestry.

It is not the purpose nor would it be possible to give the accounts for the following years in detail as many items are repeated many hundred times, but notice will be taken of all items of interest. Thus in the same year 1774.

Making three shirts	1	6
Veal and butter for Ellings wife sick		7¾
Three yards striped Dowlas	4	0
(Dowlas was a course linen).		
Tho. Elling a Loaf and four calves feet	1	4
Two-and-a-half yards of Beggar Lace		5
Irish cloth	2	2
(An early woolen cloth used for linings)		
A Loaf and a breast of lamb	1	4
Mutton, turnips, sugar and faggot and candles for Elling's wife.	1	9
John Snow going to Tinmouth		3
A Blind Man going into Devonshire		6

Poor people who wished to travel received a licence from a Magistrate in their home town which entitled them to ask for assistance in all parishes they passed through. Travellers journeying alone received 3d or 6d as noted above, while families might receive up to 1/6. Most travellers passing through Lymington were going to other ports along the coast.

"A poor Woman going to Cornwall"		6
Paid for Betty Nash Child (burial) as follows:—		
Mr. Wimbolt	1	6
Mr. Pitt	2	6
Bran and Wool		5
Beer	2	0
Total	6	5

Mr. Wimbolt was the Vicar at the time and Mr. Pitt the Parish Clerk. By act of Parliament everyone had to be buried in wool and it was the custom of the period to supply large quantities of beer and wine—for a child's funeral 2/– was a large amount as beer was 1d or 2d a pint.

To strike a more cheerful note the next item reads:—

Tobacco and Snuff (for the House)	4	0

This must have made life a little easier for these poor people and is a monthly item.

To the Turnpike for the Carriage of Coals	1	1½
To a Castaway Sailor		6
To Mrs. Bowler for the delivery of Mrs. Hart	5	0

(This was the standard payment to a Midwife)

A few more prices of interest:—

Two Coloured shirts for Beer and Johnson	6	1
A coloured Apron for Ann Curl	1	10½
A Camblet Gound for E. Edwards	7	2
A pair of Shoes	2	6
Stockings: 1 pair	2	8
1 lb Candles		7½

Something a little different:—

To Ann Keeping for combing the Childrens Heads	1	0
To a Coat and Waistcoat for Jacob Colborne	12	6
For carrying Tho's Pew to the Workhouse	1	0

(Showing that the sedan chair was in use in Lymington)

Further expenses showing the cost of "removals"—

Going to Ringwood with Hannah Cooper and to Fordingbridge with Ann Stent	1	0	3
To Turnpikes and Driver..		4	6
Six brooms			6
To Sankey for 1 weeks lodging for Mrs. Hill			9
To Mrs. Bower learning the children to read		1	0
To a spinning wheel for Mrs. Woolfry		3	0

Every effort was made to keep admissions to the House as low as possible and widows were often supplied with a spinning wheel to this end.

To Thomas Thirle for bleeding Eliz. Haines	6

Thomas Thirle was a local barber who not only undertook bleeding but acted as dentist for the same fee.

The years account ends in Easter week 1775, on the credit side of the Account £13 16s. 9¾d was handed over by the late Overseers from the previous year; sundry small credits amount to £14 14s. 7d and £490 16s. 9d. was collected by ten 3d. rates during the year bringing the total to £519 8s 1¾d—and the disbursements were £503 0s 10¼d.

1775.

½pt. wine for James Drover		6

This item appears with some frequency in the accounts, being prescribed for the sick. Wine was cheap and plentiful in the town at this period being brought in by the local ships that carried our salt to Newfoundland, thence with a cargo of fish to Spain and Portugal where wine was loaded for England.

To Capt. Blake with Beere and Apprentice	2	10	0
To expenses with do.		2	0

The last item suggests that a good deal of persuasion was necessary before the Overseer could get the apprentice off his hands.

The dreaded smallpox has now once more appeared.

Kittiers family in the smallpox	3	1	3
Elmes family in the smallpox	5	9	5½
Eliz. Badcock attending at the Pest House		5	0
To expenses going to Alton after Flight	2	7	10

Flight appears to have lived up to his name by deserting his wife and family, the account does not confirm that he was found but we must conclude that this is doubtful—as his wife appears on the list of recipients of out relief until July 1778.

November 23rd 1775.

At a Vestry held this day pursuant to an Order of the Committee of the 14th instant it was Agreed that a Letter be sent to Doctor Mason of the Fish Ponds near Bristol to know his Terms for taking in Patients Disordered in Mind in Order to try to effect a cure.

December 19th.

Ordered and Agreed that William Cake be put Apprentice to Mr. Saint with a reserve that if the fits should return on him with more violence so as to render him incapable of business he be again taken into the Poorhouse.

The only list of the Poorhouse committee appears in this year (1776) and this is recorded as follows:

(1) Joseph Hackman	(13) Willm. Rogers
(2) John Fiander	(14) James Beeston
(3) Richard Sheppard	(15) Willm. Bay
(4) William Newell	(16) John Miller
(5) John Hannaford	(17) James Gibbs
(6) Hugh Pearson	(18) John Rickman Junr.
(7) John Hart	(19) John Sparrow Senr.
(8) William Coward	(20) Henry Fricker

(9) George White
(10) Robert Lillington
(11) John Taylor
(12) Saml. Colborne Junr.

(21) Joseph Wickinden
(22) Willm. Cooper
(23) James Newell

With such a large and no doubt vigilant committee we may be sure that there was little likelihood that the Ratepayers money was wasted.

The Eling family are still a charge on the Poor Rate.

November 12th.

Farmer Amsbury be allow'd Twenty shillings to buy Clothing for Eling's Daughter at Bewley to fit her out for Service.

It is of some interest to notice the cost of fuel at this period.

	£	s	d
To Saml. Sheppard for 5 Bush of Coals		5	0

Mr. Trattle is sent to Winchester on Parish business and such is the condition of the road that a days journey only carries him as far as Redbridge.

	£	s	d
To expenses Redbridge		7	10
„ „ at Winchester	1	2	6
„ „ at Redbridge		6	10
„ „ Turnpikes		2	0
To the Chaise driver		4	0
To Mr. Trattle	5	5	0

An obituary in those times.

	£	s	d
To a woman for sitting up with Mrs. Masters three days and three nights		3	0
To the affidavit and wool		2	6
A Coffin for Mrs. Masters		10	0

The parish in the role of fairy godmother

	£	s	d
To a Licence for Marrying Isaac Dorey	2	2	0
To the Minister and Clerk		15	6
To the Ring and a Dinner		18	6

1777, May 6th.

Ordered that those Innkeepers or Alehousekeepers within this Parish that have Kettle Alleys be informed that if they suffer any Gaming in those Alleys or Cockfighting on their premises it is the determination of the Committee to use their influence with the Justices to take away their Licences.

To a poor Man from America with a Pass	1	0
To a 100 and a half of faggots for the House	12	0
To girdles for the Poor in the House	7	6
To a pair of Spectacles	1	6
Three women from America with a pass to Portsmouth	1	6

The Smallpox has again broken out.

To Mrs. Woolfrey for her child in ye Smallpox		5	0
Expenses going round to the Inoculators		1	0
To Ann Bishop for her children in ye Smallpox	1	1	0
To Dolly Buckett for attending Mrs. Miles in the Smallpox three weeks at 7/– per week	1	1	0
To different people for relief in the Smallpox	2	2	3

(and there are many other references of a like nature. There were in all twenty six deaths in this outbreak).

To James Newell to redeem his shirt	3	4

1778, November 3rd.
Inventory of Virtue Evans's Cloths etc.,—

Cash	1	3
A silver Tea Spoon	1	6
A stripe silk handk.	2	0
2 Shifts	4	0
A calico sheet	4	0
A muslin handk.	2	0
5 Caps and a calico handk.	2	6
A silk gown	7	6
An old silk gown	1	6
A red cloke old	1	3
A good petty coat	5	0
4 other old petty coats	4	0
A Blk silk bonnet	1	0
A Box	1	1

Ordered by the Committee that the above Goods be delivered to Wm. Beer for his Daughters use on his paying for her expences being in the Poorhouse and funeral charges £3 3s. 0d.

1779.

To Thomas Skeats for his substitute in the Militia	4	10	0
A pair of Patterns for Sarah Sheppard		1	2

This is the only occasion recorded in the Parish books of the supply of Patterns from the rates.

Another short obituary.

Mrs. Redman in her illness	3	0
Wine and biscuit at her funeral		5

1780.

It is agreed that if any of the Poor within the Poorhouse be seen about the Streets or elsewhere without a Ticket from the Master of the House, his pay be taken off for the week.

In this case a Ticket means a piece of paper or card with the letters L P for identification.

Also ordered that if James Alexander do not contribute towards the Maintenance of his child, that the parish will endeavour to get him on board a Man of War.

One years Insurance on the House	6	0

As a further instance of the varied assistance given by the Overseers the following is a good example.

It is this evening agreed to advance Ten or Twenty shillings to prevent Wm. Veal's Bed being sold.

4 pairs of coarse stockings	4	8

Distressed travellers of many nationalities passed through the town during this and suceeding years but the worthy Overseers were sometimes defeated as to nationality.

To a strange woman in distress	1	0

Various regiments were from time to time passing through or were quartered here and the wives often came as well.

To the wife of a soldier in the Surrey Militia for necessaries for lying in ..	10	6

1781, March 20th.

It is this evening ordered that the cottage formerly built by James Hill under shore be deemed a Nuisance and be immediately *erased* and destroyed.

March 21st.

To Mr. Rickman for pulling down Hill's House by Order of the Committee ..	10	6
To a soldier for removing the rubbish at Hill's House	3	0

There seems to have been commendable promptitude in carrying out this order.

To a brass skillet for the house	4	0

The number of children indentured between 1700–1773 is given at 141.

From Vestry Book No. 3.

1781, August 16th. Mrs. Haskell ¼ lb chocolate		1	3
This is the only time that this delicacy is mentioned in these Account Books.			
1782 March 23rd. To Misses Redman for their house	10	10	0
To Misses Redman at executing the Deed		2	6

On the same date—March 23rd, the following entry appears on the credit side of the A/c.

Received of Redman's Daughters	2	1	6
Of Ditto for their brother John Redman's part of the house which is to be paid him by the Overseers, be whom they may, when he executes ye Deed	2	12	6

1781, June 26th.

It is this evening ordered and agreed that Mrs. Southy be taken into the *lower* Almshouse and be allowed 2/6d per week till otherwise ordered.

This lower Almshouse is probably the 1st house at the foot of Union Hill which as far as can be ascertained was one of the two houses left to the Parish by Miss Burrard of Walhampton.

1782, May 7th.

Agreed that all common players of Interludes or other entertainment of the stage or any part therein, not being authorised by Law, shall be prosecuted as Vagrants if they presume to act in any part of the Town.

1782, Rebecca Bucketts Story.

Spent going to Mrs. Skinner with Rebecca Buckett			7
Mr. Rutter for his boat to Portsmouth on Rebecca Bucketts a/c.	1	1	0
Mr. Foot for removing Rebecca Buckett in the chair to the House. ..		1	6
To beer for Rebecca Bucket at *The Angel*			2½
Mrs. How (midwife) for Rebecca Buckett		5	0
Still more strangers are seen in Lymington.			
To Seven Portugese with a pass to Southampton		3	6
To Mrs. Edwards for making a Gown		1	6

March 26th.

It is this evening agreed to allow Thomas Kitch one guinea to assist him in paying his substitute to serve in the Militia.

1782, April 20th.

To Saml. Collings in part for curing the Distemper in the House	1	1	0
Expenses attending six Vagrants to Justice with the Constables		3	10

June 17th,

To twelve Sailors with a pass		6	0

Harts story in brief

August 5th, Attending Mrs. Hart at Milford	1	0
„ „ Mr. Blake for his cart to ditto	2	3
„ „ To Mrs. Hart	1	6
August, 7th Spent attending Mrs. Hart to Milford		6
„ „ To Mr. Smee for his Chaise and the Turnpike	2	9

August 8th Spent going to Yarmouth after Hart   8   4½
To Mr. Webster for his Boat   6   0
  „   „   To Mr. Bevis to carry Hart on Board the Ship   10   6
  „   „   To Warder and Thirle for a Boat to go aboard   2   6
  „   „   To Expenses at Yarmouth   1   0   6

It will be noticed that Thirle besides his duties of drawing teeth, cutting hair and bleeding was also available as a constable when required.

This affair cost the Parish £2 15s. 10½d but it would be of some interest to know the items £1 0s. 6d. spent at Yarmouth.

1783.

To a poor Woman in distress by fire   1   0
Mr. Thirle for drawing a tooth for Mary Sheppard   6
½ bushel of Coals   6

1783.

July 7th.
To a feather bed and bed tick for the House 1 14   0
July 13th.
To a Sailor with one arm, a wife and two children—going to Plymouth   ..   1   0
To Phillis Uppell one week nursing Mistress Norris   2   6
October 13th. Times may have been hard, but this hardly seems adequate.
To three Sailors in distress   6

1784.

To three Sailors cast away at the back of the Island   1   0
To the Club at *The Angel* for Haysom to save him from being excluded   ..   3   0
Biscuits for Maceys family in the Smallpox   6
An Hourglass for ditto   10

1784.

A new bedstead with a sacking bottom   18   6
To George Ware one years House rent for How's family   2   8   2
Showing the extremely low rent of a small house and three items showing the current prices.
To one dozen spoons for the House   2   0
Bought for Maceys family 11¾ lbs Bakon at 7½d   7   4
27¼ lbs. Veal   9   2

1785.

November 8th.

It is agreed to allow Samuel Sheppard one guinea to carry Capt. Hibbard to the Infirmary at Salisbury and 5/– to provide for the Captain on the Road.

This was evidently one of our sea Captains who had fallen on hard times, his family had been receiving help for some months.

Sam Sheppard lived in New Street opposite what is now the Literary Institute and appears to have been a general carrier as he was often employed by the Overseers.

1786.

William Hibberd to carry him to Bath	18	0
To beer etc., for him		9

This is quite an extraordinary expenditure, it appears to have been a farewell party.

The next entry shows that even Overseers had kind hearts.

To Mrs. Miller for beer for the poor at Easter	11	0
Beer at 2½d per pint gives 53 adults in the House at this time.		
To Hill's Children turned out of doors	1	0
Expended on two Lascans in provisions and cash	3	5
Expenses re Sailor killed belonging to the Timber Hoy	10	2½
Jos Winsey going for the Coroner (Winchester)	14	0
Expenses with the Coroner and Jury at Mr. Bays (*The Ship* inn)	17	9

1787.

To bread, candles, butter, ale, brandy and sundry other articles at different times for Pitt in the Smallpox		9	9½
Coals for ditto		3	8
Moses Kittier on leaving the House to go to Pool for Newfoundland ..		5	0

One wonders why he had to start from Poole as boats were leaving Lymington with salt every month for the Newfoundland fisheries.

Lost on Light Gold	1	6	9½
A woman sick at Ingrams		14	9

Travellers on foot taken ill on the road would take refuge in the barns and outhouses of the first inn in the town which was *The Blacksmith's* (now *The Hearts of Oak*).

Altering the ironwork of the stocks		11
John Braxton for new stocks	18	9

Hardly an expense for the Overseers but one that the Mayor and burgesses should have undertaken.

November 20th.

That Woolfrey's Girl have a spinning turn given her.

1787.

That Mary Hart, Ann Wassill, Frances Eling and Mary Stretch be obliged to work at the weaving turn from 6 o'clock in the morning till 8 at night. That Jane Bailey do learn the children to read and knit. That Eliz. Draper do spin the whole day. That Widow Curtis be taken into the Poor House unless she can support herself out—at 1/- per week.

1788.
December 4th.

It was proposed that the parishes of Boldre, Brockenhurst, Beaulieu and Lymington should combine to build one common Workhouse but when put to the vote it was negatived by Lymington by 58 votes to nil. It was not until 48 years later in 1836 that this amalgamation took place and the present house was built to become known as the Lymington Union.

Cost; £4,500; Architect—Mr. S. Kempthorne.

1788.
December 11th.

At a Vestry meeting held this day in our Parish Church to take into consideration the state of the Workhouse belonging to this Parish (it being found too small for the purpose designed). It is therefore ordered by this Vestry that a survey be made of the said home in order to the enlarging the same.

This Vestry do therefore appoint

Mr. Charles St. Barbe.	Mr. John Woodford
Mr. Henry Foreman	Mr. Thomas Lavington
Mr. Jas Brixey	Mr. John Sheppard
Mr. Richard Hayward	Mr. John Newell
Mr. Wm. Bay	Mr. Wm. Kent
Mr. Jas Gibbs	Mr. Thos Colborne
Mr. Robert Lillington	Mr. Wilson Bays
Mr. Thos. Badcock	

to inspect the same and to report what is necessary to be done at a future Vestry to be summoned for that purpose.

The Plan for this work was put before a meeting held on January 8th, 1789 and finally passed at a subsequent meeting on January 15th.

1789.

On May 28th Mr. William Tarver was unanimously appointed Master of the Poor House at a salary of £25 per annum and it was at the same time agreed that his two youngest children be admitted into the Poor House with him and his wife.

1789.

July 9th.

The Robert Parsons be allowed 30/– towards his learning to play the Violin as by that means its presumed he will be able to support himself, as he being affected with blindness, he is rendered incapable of doing anything else towards his maintenance.

1790.

Lymington, March 11th.

At a vestry meeting held this day in our parish Church (according to a public notice given the preceeding Sunday) to take into Consideration a proposal of several persons for a general innoculation for the smallpox throughout this parish.

We whose names are here unto subscribed do on mature deliberation entirely condemn the said proposal as believing if such a scheme was to be adopted it would on every account be attended with consequences highly injurious to this parish.

Signed; 2 Churchwardens, 1 Overseer and 21 Parishioners.

1790.

April 6th.

The Surgeon's allowance was agreed at 12 guineas a year.

Orders of Vestry 1791.

June 2nd Whereas since the enlargement of the Poor House of this parish, the necessary houses belonging to the same, have by their being situated so near the workroom, become a very great nuisance to the same. And whereas the Windows in the Work room are found insufficient for conveying light to all parts of the said room. Therefore at a Vestry meeting held this day in our Parish Church to take the same into consideration, it is ordered by this Vestry that the Necessary houses before mentioned be forthwith removed from the place where they now stand to a greater distance from the dwelling house, and that the place thought most elegible for that purpose is adjoining to the Hogs Stys of the said Poor House. And also that the paling be continued around the Hogs Stys as these continuing open, is a nuisance to the public in general. And also it is ordered that two new windows be added to the North side of the said Room.

1791.

The reign of Mr. & Mrs. Tarver was however of short duration as we read on February 17th.

Whereas many complaints have been made against the conduct of the present Master and Mistress of the Poor House of this parish and therefore at a Vestry Meeting held this day in our Parish Church in order to take the sense of the parish on the dismissal of the present Master and Mistress from their said office at Lady Day next it is agreed by the persons assembled at this present meeting that it shall be determined by the Majority of Votes.

Thirty nine voted for dismissal, fifteen voted against.

On March 10th of the same year Mr. James Salter of Downton, Wiltshire, and his wife were appointed to this office at a salary of £20 and 2/6d out of every £1 which the poor shall earn in the House but if the same shall not amount to £25 the parish shall then make up the deficiency.

1791.

Lymington, February 4th.

Whereas the smallpox has broke out in several poor families belonging to this parish and there are great reasons to suppose that many more are infected with the said disorder, at a vestry meeting held this day in our parish Church it was proposed that a general innoculation should immediately commence throughout the parish, but as there appears to be different opinions concerning the same, the Churchwardens and Overseers do hereby put the same to the vote in order to collect the general sense of the parish on that subject.

For Innoculation twenty three. Against fourteen.

Note: The number innoculated by Mr. Beckley was about 300, of whom two died. Mr. Nike about 300, of whom eighteen died. Mr. Dolland about 500, of whom not one died.

1794.

In 1794 a Manufactury was set up for the proper employment of the able poor and a man with the singularly appropriate name of Henry Foreman was appointed as the Inspector at twenty guineas per annum.

To give but one instance of the earnings of the poor from this and other means in the year 1800:—

The sale of Mops produced	90	10	9½
Spinning Worsted and Knitting	21	17	5½
Outdoor Work	41	6	6½
	£153	14	9½

The Rates in this year were:

20 collections of 3d in the £1 totalling £1265 14 2

1802.

October 1st, 1795.

It was agreed this day that an addition to the North side of the Work House, be carried into execution according to a plan produced at this Vestry.

Overseers A/Cs 1795.

	£	s	d
Two women and children with pass for Portsea, two nights in Town ..		2	6
Paid. Langley, Oram and Sanger of Sarum £3 each with their apprentices ..	9	0	0
For filling up Indentures for the above		7	6
Spent with the above Masters		5	0
And allowed expenses (transport)		5	0
To the three girls			6
Four pairs of Indentures	2	18	6
Filling up one pair		2	6

Note: Langley Oram and Sanger appear in the following month as suppliers to the House £15 probably wool—and this probably points to a business deal, as it is very seldom that children were indentured outside the parish hence the increase from £2 to £3.

	£	s	d
One pair Handcuffs		3	6
To two men passing to Liverpool		1	0
Paid of scribbling cards		4	6
Two men cleaning the Well		2	6
Sinking a well		2	6
Beer		1	0
Bricks		2	6
ditto		6	0
Bathing R. Green ten times		2	6
Obedeal Newill for a Plan		3	0
Writing proposals for ye new additions		2	6

Note: this was addition to the North side of the House see Vestry order for Oct: 1st 1795.

	£	s	d
Spent with ye Officers and Workman about ye new additions to the workhouse		3	6
13½ Bushels of Grains at 5d per Bushel		5	7½
(now 14/– per bushel)			
Rabbit			8
Two Pigs Henges		1	10
("Plucks" = Heart, liver and lungs 23/4)			
Half years wash to Mr. Rice		2	0
Pair of Trowers to Samuel Abbott		2	0
Coffin for Francis Eling		10	0
(Now about £8.00)			
Bearers		2	0
Parson and Clerk		4	0
Geneva 1 point		1	8

Note: Geneva is a spirit distilled from grain flavoured with juniper berries (Hollands Gin).

	£	s	d
To Foot at ye "Bells" for a woman in distress		1	6

12 Pewter spoons	2	6
Eight wooden spoons		8
James Rawlings for killing two pigs	4	0
A jacket for Frampton	5	6

1796.

Sam Bannister ten days work at 10d		8	4
Brandy for Men emptying the Privy		1	6
For a well crook and pole		1	8
Two Holdfasts for the House			6
Constable apprehending a vagrant		5	0
To an American woman and three children		1	6
Getting them out of town		3	0
Two calves heads and two Gullies		5	0
A poor man from French prison		1	0
To an American sailor		1	0
To the Old Town Jury		1	0
Spent with the Officers of Rumsey		6	0
One Bushel of Salt		6	6
Paid five volunteers for the Parish at £10 10s. 0d. each	52	10	0
To expenses on a/c of the above	6	10	11

1797.

Two Loads Gravel		2	6
Bottle of bathing spirits			9
To Horse hire and 1d the Bridge etc.		2	0
Received by a Dividend on shares 5 Guinea Note	1	11	6
Spent at the Bugle at receiving the Books		15	0
Spent getting lodging for six Turks		1	0
Expenses clearing the town of vagrants		2	6

26th March, 1799.

At a Vestry meeting held this day and adjourned to the House of Mr. Robert Taylor being the Sign of the Bugle in this parish, Mr. William Huse, Vestry Clerk be allowed £2 2s. 0d. in addition to his former salary of £5 5s. 0d. on increase of duties, and Mr. James Bartlett Parish Clerk an addition of £2 2s. 0d. for the same reason.

1801.

Vestry Clerks Salary increased to 10 guineas.
Surgeons Salary £16 16s. 0d.
June 18th Robbery of Workhouse Garden of Cabbages = £5 5s. 0d. reward offered.

1802.

The meeting of February 25th was adjourned to the House of Mrs. Rachael Robinson at the Sign of the Anchor and Hope.

Mr. James Bartlett, Parish Clerk, salary £10 10s 0d. p.a.

September 23rd The Masters wife Elizabeth Salter having died, The Vestry appointed Susanna Woodman as Mistress of the said workhouse.

Master's salary stated to be £24 p.a. plus 2/6 in £ on the poor's earnings.

It is therefore ordered that the said Susanna Woodman, shall receive out of the said sum of £24 paid to James Salter the sum of £8 p.a.

April 12th 1803. Vestry Meeting held at the Parish Church.

Mr. John Ryale appointed surgeon.

Rev. Mr. Homes to be allowed one guinea for the soil of the Churchyard.

1798.

1 doz. lbs. Salt Butter	9	0
Paid for 2 cwt. 3 qrs. 12 lbs. Old junk	10	0
To the wife, child of Wheeler committed to prison for sedition practices ..	3	0
To bad copper received from late Overseers being collected by Mr. Bartlett in the course of last year	16	6
To a soldier's wife coming out of smallpox. 1	1	0
A quarters quit rent for a cottage at Buckland	1	0
Mr. John Mitchell of Newport for 3 gallons of Mint water for the Poor House	11	10
Receiving the Books	15	0
(Supper at *The Red Lion*)		
Nails and Virrils	10	0

1799

To Lucy Bracker to be married	4	0
To Gales wife to assist her in repairing her house, injured by the frost ..	6	0
A pair of specticals for Sarah Barnes	2	0
Spent at *The Red Lion* receiving the books 1	1	0

1800.

Expenses removing Kerby's family to Yewern:		
Paid Mr. John Mitchell Horse 1	1	0
Paid Sam Collins Cart and Horse 1	3	6
Expended at Christchurch	5	0
„ „ Wimborne 1	4	6

Expended at Blandford	1	0	3
„ „ Turnpikes			10
	£4	15	1
Postage on a Dble letter from Bath		1	0
Mr. Norris for an Oxes Head		3	0
Samuel Elgar for a coffin for Gafs Ackleton		10	0
5 cwt. 3 qrs. 5 lbs. Cheese at 73/–	21	2	8

Paid to Ann Herbert the wife and one child of Peter Herbert substitute for
Abraham Armstrong of the parish of St. Giles in the town of Reading in
the County of Berks of nine days the time the Regt. was in the Isle of
Wight by Order of Percival Lewis Esq.

Wight by Order of Percival Lewis Esq.		3	0
Hezekiah Hinks lived on Town Hill wife two sons and two daughters			
Wine for John Young's Family in the smallpox		2	0
To Percival Lewis Esq. with his apprentice	2	0	0
Mr. Salters salary for the quarter	6	0	0
Mr. Salters poundage on £23 19s. 10d.	3	0	0
Wine 3/3, Milk 8/9, Butter for the Month 10/–	1	2	0
To the Cryer for crying respecting robbing the Garden		1	0
Mr. John Blake for Flour (one month)	21	16	0
Mr. John Lejenne Ditto	10	10	0
Mr. St. Barle five chaldren Coals	10	5	0
To a French Woman		1	0
To the Constable to the Assizes		12	0
A poor sailor		1	0
A pint of wine for Linsay's wife		2	0
Nicholas Read in the palsy		7	6
53 lbs of Beef at 6d. lb.			
Farmer Olding for 38 lbs wool at 5d.		15	10
For Chaise to Burley and Winchester	1	2	6
Postage to and from Plymouth to Clerk of S. H. Militia			9
To four Americans		2	0
24 lbs. Rice		12	0
(now 30/–)			
800 plants of Beach 5/4 500 Plants of Turgis		3	4
Three Wounded sailors		2	0
Six Bushels of grains		3	0
2 lbs. sugar for Rice Puddings		1	8
A bottle of port wine for an old Woman		3	4

By Cash Received for Mops	90	10	9½
„ „ Outdoor work	41	6	6½
„ „ Spinning Worsted and Knitting	21	17	5½
20 Rates of 3d.	1265	14	2

1801.

Expenses at receiving the Books		15	0
48½ lbs. Veal (per Moses Pedler at 6d.)	1	4	3
For a chair (sedan) to convey Ann Young to the Poor House		2	0
20 sacks of Potatoes	4	10	0
To three Maltese in distress		2	0
For the burial of a child of the Dutch		4	0
Cash expended on 41 women and children etc. wives of soldiers belonging to 85 Regt, who were left in the parish, when Regt. marcht	7	11	0

1802.

Expenses at *The Rose* on a/c of R. Holly		2	8
To the Drummer of the 35th per order		13	0
5 cwt. Cheese at 52/6 (May Fair)	13	2	6
Spent on Receiving the Books	1	0	0
Messenger for the Coroner for man killed by waggon		15	0
2 Bags of potatoes at 3/6 (now 17/–) 10 Bushels of Barley at 3/9 (now 13/– bushel)	1	17	6

1803.

Paid Constable per order of the Justice for apprehending four vagabonds	1	0	0
Received of the Treasurer of the County in full for wives of the Militia Men	18	19	0
By cash of Mr. Benjamin Drawbridge, Mr. Butcher. Mr. Thomas, Mr. Morris and Mr. Andrew Hobbs excused apprentice	40	0	0
Paid for Wooden leg for J. Bampton		1	2
5 or 6 cwt of cheese bought twice a year at May and October Fairs.			
November 11th 1802 George Gordon		1	0
July 1803. Paid for the History of George Gordon written by himself dedicated to Parish of Lymington		1	9
24 lbs Fish		8	0
To William Tarver half of £13 7s. 0d. being the average price of a substitute in supplementing Militia	6	13	6
A load of wheat was purchased 4 to 6 weeks at approx.	12	0	0
For an Ass for Robert Parsons		12	0
James Gerrard, for taking care of the Engine and Buckets and providing oil for the same, allowed	1	11	6

"This meeting is herby adjourned to the House of Mr. Jarvis Harker bearing the sign of *The Anchor and Hope* ".

July 7th, 1803.

At a Vestry assembled this day for the purpose of taking into consideration the best manner of raising the number of men which might be levied on this parish to furnish the Army of Reserve.

But as we are not in possession of the Act of Parliament passed for that purpose, it is therefor agreed to adjourn this meeting to Monday 11th July at 6 o'clock to take the same into further consideration.

July 11th 1803. At a Vestry Meeting held this day pursuant to the above adjournment, there being only one parishioner present the Business is finally dropt.

January 19th 1804.

We whose names are hereunto subscribed being Householders in the Parish etc. do hereby agree to become special Constables in case of an attempt by the Enemy to invade this Country and be subject in all respects to the Control and Direction of the Civil Magistrate.

Wm. Lyne, John Rickman, David Dove, John Blake, Samuel Dixon, Edw. Templar, Benj. Elgar, Andrew Hobbs, Thos. Elmes, John Day.

1803.

	£	s	d
Expenses incurred on a/c of Geo Gordon for Cloaths, carriage etc. and admittance into Bethlem Hospital	8	2	10
John Colborne and seven others for substitute in Army of Reserve at £10 each	80	0	0
A New Copper Furnace wt. 43¾ lbs. at 2/–	4	7	6
Less old ditto wt. 37 lbs. at 10d.	1	10	10
	2	16	8

1804.

	£	s	d
Pd. Gale three days work in Garden		4	6
Window Tax		3	0
Pd. Mr. Groves for Leeches		2	0

April 3rd 1804.

James Bartlett, Parish Clerk salary raised to 20 guineas for collecting poor rates instead of 6 guineas as heretofore in consideration of the assistance of Mr. Bartlett in the Office of Overseer.

July 18th 1805.

It is ordered that Overseers pay to Samuel Collins £2 2s. 0d. on account of the removal of Nicholas Jenkins and family into Cornwall over and above what was agreed on, it having been found that He had a great many more Miles to travel and of consequence being two days more from Home.

April 13th 1809.

Thomas Daw of Kings Somborne appointed Master of the House.

April 28th 1809.

New Poor Law Act of George 3rd. Guardian's (James Bartlett) Salary ..   21   0   0
Master or Governor £24 plus one eighth of the earnings of the Poor.

In 1810.

Guardian 25 guineas.
Master, £35 plus one eighth.

1814.

Guardian £21.
Master £35 plus one eighth.

1815.

Mr. Wm. Dixon elected Vestry Clerk.

1805.

	£	s	d
Expenses to London to apprehend Wm. Parker for deserting his family ..	11	0	0
Irish Jack 2/6, 1/–, 3/–, (7 days).			
For Chaise to Gosport	1	8	0
Keep of Horse		9	0
Expended in going to Gosport	1	7	0
For a Vessel to Cowes and Southampton	1	5	0
Paid Mr. Bevis a Boat to the I. of Wight		15	0

1806.

	£	s	d
Thirteen sacks of wheat	23	8	0
A Bedstead		6	6
Eight sacks wheat at £17 10s. pd.	14	0	0
Paid for straw for Thatching the Pest House	1	7	6
Paid to Capt: Wm. Oake Conduct Money	2	2	0
Of the Countess of Delawarr a fine to be excused an Apprentice	10	0	0
Messenger to Winton for the Coroner on a/c of one of the Depot who shot himself		15	0
To Ann Young for instructing Children to Knitt Gloves	3	3	0
Expenses on a/c of Henry Bladwin's wife in smallpox and burying her ..	5	4	6
Mr. Judd a chaise to Gosport	2	5	0
Messrs. McIlwain and Noake journey to Coliton to remove Rawings ..	22	2	9
Harker & Bartlett to London to remove Johnson's Family	13	4	0

1808.

To Hampton and Braker for Mudwall at Gales House—in part	..	..	1 1 0
Paid Building Gales House			14 0
Paid Mr. Noake for straw for thatching Gales House			4 1 0

1809.

A poor man sick at *The Six Bells*		1 6
Two Women from a French prison		1 6
Sick woman at *The Bells*		2 6

1810.

R. Peckham for 300 Bavins	1	7 0
13 Sacks of wheat	39	0 0

1811.

For thatching the pest House		6 3
Expenses at taking the population of the Parish	2	19 0

1812.

In House 77; Out Door 36; Occasional 34.

1802.

23 Males; 41 Females (30 employed in Manufacture).
Outdoor 1782, 24; 1800, 80; 1812, 36; 34 occasional.

1813.

Paid Miss Huse for taking Sarah Braken, an apprentice to be instructed in Mantua making	3	3 0
(Mantua=Ladys' cloaks)		

1814.

A Forged Bank note returned £2. 0s. 0d.

Paid Mr. Norris (*The Ship*) for beer for the poor in the House on the day of Thanksgiving		16 0
Mr. Judd on a/c of the Prosecution of Mr. Souper and others for Murder ..	20	14 5
Paid Mr. H. Green, Coroner of County, expenses for prosecution for Murder	11	2 2
Received for a watch, left by a man who died at Chipps		16 0

1815.

800 Bavins at 18/–	7	4 0
A poor family at *The Blacksmiths Arms*.		8 6

1816.

May 2nd. To the Rt. Hon. the Secretary of State for the Home Department.

The humble respectful Memorial of the Overseers of the Poor and others, Inhabitants of the Parish of Lymington, Hants, paying Poor's rates, in Vestry assembled herewith:—

That your Memorialists have for twenty years past been at great Expense in supporting Foreigners, their wives and children not having any legal settlement, which has been occasioned by the Depot for Foreign Troops having been in the said Parish.

That at the Removal of the said Depot these numbers so much increased, a List being herewith transmitted as to amount—to more than one fourth of the Poor in the Parochial Poor House. That the expected return of the Royal Foreign Artillery from the West Indies and other circumstances render it probable that the burden will be still further increased.

That those of your Memorialists upon whom the principal charge of the Poor Rates fall are Tenants at high Rents and that the Parish is otherwise much burdened with Poor. Your Memorialists therefore humbly and respectfully trust that his Majesty's Government will take the hardship of their case into Consideration, and afford them such relief as in their wisdom they may judge that the case requires.

1816.

	£	s	d
1000 Herrings		10	0
To two Prussians		1	0
Mr. R. Badcock for Sanpenberg's passage	3	2	0
Cutting up a Pig			6

1817.

	£	s	d
Expenses of Scotch Betty to London	2	0	0
Spent at *The Red Lion*, 25th March	6	8	11

1818.

	£	s	d
List shoes for Wid Swift		2	6
NOTE List=made of strips of woolen selvage.			
Paid Capt. Williams to take Robert West to Liverpool	2	2	0
Boat hire to vessel with R. West		3	0

1819.

	£	s	d
Fine to Coroner for not discovering the Murder of a Child		13	4
Expenses of Mrs. Hartman inside of Coach from Winchester		12	0
NOTE Mrs. Hartman had been taken to Winchester Hospital two months before.			
Four Bushels of Salt at 16/3	3	5	0
Man driving Pigs from Ringwood		4	0
Paid Russell at *The True Blue* for Board Lodging to John Gass's wife.	1	0	0

	£	s	d
Received: Fines of three Landlords	1	10	0
Received: Fines from Gerrard, Harris, Powman, Golding and Ivaney being found in a public House on the Sabbath at 3/4		16	8

1820.

	£	s	d
Paid Capt. Hoar to take woman and child to Ireland	1	1	0
Provisions for ditto	1	8	0
1 ton 7 cwt of Cheese bought this year at 56/– cwt.	76	0	0
Straw for the Blind House		3	0

1821.

	£	s	d
Paid G. Bran sawing 168 ft. Elm Boards at 4/– 100 ft.		6	5

1823.

	£	s	d
Paid to *The True Blue* for a sick man (John Taylor)	1	17	0

1824.

	£	s	d
Paid a woman sick at *The Blacksmiths Arms*		6	0
Six shipwrecked men		6	0
Paid Coachhire and Coachman conveying Rd. Whitehead and family from Lymington to Huntingdon and Guardian from Hunt. to Lym.	17	1	0
Expenses of Journey	1	12	10

1825.

	£	s	d
Paid Joseph Cruitt and I. Lawrence carrying Harry Lane to Church, there not being sufficient men in the Poor House able.		2	6
A sick woman at *The True Blue* and Lodging seven days		7	0
Boys and Girls at the Poor House for their use at the Fair by Order of the Vestry		10	0
Three Bushels of Salt		3	0
Paid on a Light Guinea received by Mr. Newman		1	0
Richard Hutchins with apprentice	12	0	0
(later to £15).			

1826

	£	s	d
John Baverstock for his trouble driving Cow to Southampton Fair		10	0
Received of Phillip Edmonds fine for swearing before the Bench of Magistrates		1	0

1852.
From Vestry Book No. 6.

No. of houses in parish (not exceeding £6 p.a.) 366
No. of houses in parish (exceeding £6 per annum). 528

894

Gross Rateable Value £15,976 8 0

Year		Houses	Population	
1801	Houses	475	Population	2378
1811	,,		,,	2641
1821	,,	526	,,	3164
1831	,,	659	,,	3361
1851	,,	865	,,	4164
1911	,,		,,	4329
1931	,,		,,	5157

A funeral procession to St Thomas' Church in 1805. Notice the position of the clock, this one dating from 1674 was replaced in 1835.

CHAPTER   SEVEN

Travel in the 18th Century

There were several coaches which left Lymington in the early days. The Telegraph from *The Anchor and Hope* Inn at 5 in the morning, and reached Southampton at 7.30. The Independent from *The Nag's Head* (Londesborough) at 5 and reached Southampton at the same time.

Nags Head Field, now Grove Gardens, was the field in which the coach and postchaise horses were let out and the paddock in the rear of *The Angel Hotel*.

The Weymouth Commercial Coach started from *The Star*, Southampton at 8 a.m. arriving at *The Anchor and Hope* at 10.30 and left again at 11 a.m. passing through Mudeford, Christchurch, Poole, Wareham and Dorchester arriving at Weymouth at 7 p.m.

WAGGONS

A waggon left for Salisbury twice a week at 9 a.m., to Christchurch three times a week at 2 p.m. To Southampton two stage waggons left twice a week, and to Ringwood once every Saturday.

COACHES AND POSTCHAISES

The word coach comes from Kotze in Hungary and was introduced into England in 1555. The old family coaches were drawn by four and sometimes six carthorses to drag them through the vile roads and footmen attended with staves to hoist the wheels along in the bad places.

In the early 1700s the wealthy travelled by their own coaches and when posting was established by postchaise to hire a postchaise cost as much as 27/– per day and a wealthy foreigner who once hired a landau and horses to tour England at this price only got as far as Oxford before the coachman refused to proceed owing to the roads being in such a bad state. The hardy Englishman frequently travelled on horseback it being a pleasant and independent way of going in summer and if the weather was good.

Bad roads and mirey patches could be avoided by cutting across fields and one saw the country at ones leisure and saved the money on the coach.

On the other hand a man riding alone was liable to be attacked by highwaymen and he must know the road otherwise he might go far out of his way and find himself benighted in a bog and he could only carry what he could cram into two saddle bags.

No person of quality travelled other than by postchaise. This vehicle became common about the middle of the century (1750). The chaise held two persons with a dickey behind for the servant. It was lighter than the old lumbering coaches and travelled at a better pace—no coachman—the horses being driven by a postboy who was mounted on one of them. They were grown men and some quite elderly—a hard life indeed exposed to wind and weather and contending with bad roads, tired horses and irritable passengers.

There were frequent complaints about them, that they were surly and drinkers and sometimes in league with the highwaymen who infested the roads.

These bandits would often have postboys in their pay and if a particularly wealthy looking gentleman was leaving an Inn, word would be sent that someone worthy of their attention would be travelling on the road at such and such an hour the following day.

The postboys wore a uniform, usually a tight jacket with braid knee breeches and a round jockey cap. They expected a tip of 3d per mile. This, with 1/6 a mile for posting and 6d for ostling every time the horses were changed became a very expensive mode of travel.

Comparing these prices with the enormous rise in costs over the past 200 years, we can agree that this form of travel was the most expensive one could undertake. The stage coach was cheaper, the charge being 2d or 3d per mile with tips at the journeys end for coachman and guard. This stage coach was a heavy lumbering vehicle and in early days was covered in leather studded with nails, the frames being picked out in colours—the windows were covered with boards or leather curtains.

They were entirely devoid of springs and lumbered along at four miles an hour or even less drawn by three horses with a postboy on one of the pair. They had two seats inside, large enough to accommodate six persons but rather crowded at that with straw on the floor for warmth. Outside they sometimes carried as many as twelve people. This crowding was the common cause for complaint as they were built to carry no more than six on top. Then there was the basket or rumble to carry luggage or passengers. Getting on and off the top had to be done in the street by a ladder for no coach could then pass through the archway of an Inn yard with outside passengers seated. Later when seats were built on top the newer Inns built arches sufficiently high to accommodate them.

The reason for travelling in this extreme discomfort was of course that it was cheap. The outsider only paid half the price of inside and could if he chose travel in the basket for the same sum.

If driven in by extreme discomfort or rain and snow he could only do so if one of the insiders agreed and he was then put next to his benefactor.

In 1783 a bill was introduced in Parliament to regulate the number of outside passengers. Only six might be carried on the roof and two on the box of a three or four horse coach and on a pair horse coach only three on the roof and one on the box.

These coaches paid a tax of £5 yearly and ½d per mile. The only recorded case of a fatal accident in Lymington was in 1784 when a person was killed by a "machine" running over him. The machine was a stage coach and the horses were called machiners.

In 1734 one of the new conveyances advertised as the Newcastle Flying Coach which did the journey to London in nine days, three days faster than any other coach. The coaches had previously gone about 25 miles a day and then stopped to rest, the passengers staying at the Inn and continuing the following day when the horses were considered sufficiently rested—now by changing horses the journey could be done quicker. The coaches too began to improve, glass taking the place of the leather curtains and later still the coaches were fitted with springs. This was a mixed blessing; the mail coaches were hung so high that the motion was often intolerable and the landlady of an Exeter Inn declared that the passengers arriving in the mails were generally so ill that they at once retired to bed without supper to the disadvantage of her house.

As I have said the old coaches had no springs and what the jolting must have been over bad roads with ruts of great depth we cannot to-day conceive. The first Mail Coach was put on the road in 1784. Before that date the mails were carried by postboys on horseback a system which was very unsatisfactory. A single sheet of paper cost 4d, every addition however made it a double letter 8d, or a treble letter 1/-. An oz weight was 1/4. Overridden horses fell lame or ill, the temptation to linger with a mug of beer over the alehouse fire in bad weather was often too great to be resisted and on lonely roads the men were often set upon and robbed. So many letters never reached their destination that people hesitated to use the post but bribed the drivers of stage coaches to carry letters although this was against the law.

The drivers and guards of the new mail coaches were armed and whatever respect and attention they may have paid to passengers the armed guard could be a terror on the roads as they sometimes shot at passing dogs, hogs, sheep and poultry and even in towns to the terror of the inhabitants. On one occasion a guard went so far as to shoot at a tollkeeper.

The old stage coach had no guards, the driver indeed had a blunderbuss concealed in the box but seldom used it. These men had low wages and depended on tips for income and parcels and letters sent by them would therefore be delivered at less than the Post Office charged. By those means the guard did fairly well and on good routes might make £400 a year, on out of the way routes fairly badly and the night coaches worst of all.

In the early days there were no night coaches and passengers were dragged out of bed at five in the morning and deposited shaking, tottering at an Inn at 9 in the evening. These night coaches were first on the road. Anything was considered good enough for them—poor horses, decayed harness and wheels which came off. No one travelled by a night coach if he could avoid it and the unfortunate driver sometimes made only 2/6d a week, 6d was the usual tip for a driver. In 1820 one local driver was named "Jockey" Beale.

Coachmen were not men to be trifled with as they sat aloft on the box clad in caped coats and fancy waistcoats sipping brandy and water brought from the Inn by obsequious attendants. In the eyes of the sporting set there was something glamorous in them and many paid extra for a seat beside the driver and would gladly pay a guinea to take the reigns along a smooth road.

For many years to about 1813 a driver named Peter Wise drove the mail from Lymington and was the chief source of news to the townsfolk during the Napoleonic wars.

A coachman was liable to a fine of £5–£10 for allowing a passenger to drive and the common informer who was so rife in the 18th century was often lurking behind the hedge.

On May Day the coaches would be decked with flowers, with holly at Christmas and at naval and military victories with laurel. The mail coaches towards the end of the century could do as much as seven miles per hour on tolerable roads but the stages did three to four miles and in bad weather even less. The stages had to stop or slow down at every tollgate while the mails, their horns playing, dashed through the gates without paying a penny.

It is said that a lady who was fond of taking country walks once decided to meet a coach at an Inn and take it part of the road home. When she reached the Inn she found that it had already passed by but by walking quickly she was able to catch it up—a stage driver would generally make room for a chance passenger and pocket the fare. In the ordinary way it was necessary to secure a seat beforehand at a booking office and this persisted into the rail way era and down to our own time.

In early days many coaches laid up for the winter emerged again on 1st of May.

When coaches had to climb a hill the male passengers got out and walked and sometimes condescended to exchange a few words with the "outsides" letting it be known that they would not speak to such low fellows when they came to the Inn.

STAGE WAGGONS

Another early means of transport was the Stage Waggon. This vehicle was an immense cart with benches inside and covered by a canvas or leather hood. It was drawn at a foots pace by eight horses and the waggoners walked at their head. It never did more than two miles an hour and only travelled in day time. Generally the same team of horses pulled the waggon through all its journey but the flying waggon changed horses. These heavy waggons cut up the roads and after 1766 they were compelled to have wheels not less than sixteen inches broad and a bonus was given to those two feet in breadth. A few years later waggons were put on the roads that had wheels so broad that they rolled the roads.

People travelled in these slow moving uncomfortable carts because they were cheap, it being 1d or 1½d a mile against 3d or 4d by stage coach. Travellers who went in their own carriages could take as much luggage as the horses could draw. The coaches limited passengers luggage to 14 lb. in weight which was carried free, anything over that was charged at 1d per pound and heavy luggage was refused. This was sent by the Waggon and the rates were high, 40/– a ton was charged for a short journey.

It was not only the poor who travelled on the stage waggons. Middle class persons, especially women travelling alone, often preferred them as the highwayman scorned them as beneath their notice.

It is true the waggons carried goods and luggage but these were usually heavy bulky articles and highwaymen on horses could not remove anything big and heavy nor could they spend the time examining luggage, it would have been too risky. Their policy was to snatch jewellery and purses from the unlucky passengers and to get away quickly.

ROAD, TOLLS ETC.

The roads were very bad in Sussex and were generally so unpassable in winter that the judges in circuit refused to hold Assizes at Lewes. They struggled down to Guildford or Horsham and waited there for the prisoners, constables and jurymen to plough up there in the mud as best they might.

In Devon there was no road west of Exeter which could be used for wheeled traffic. Early in the 18th century it was still the custom to repair the roads by statute labour and all parishioners were called on to contribute to their upkeep. The squire and farmers were obliged to send a certain number of horses and carts and labourers had to give six days work a year.

In many parishes it became the custom to accept payment in money and instead of lending his waggon the farmer or squire might pay the sum of 30/– for upkeep and in time a sort of highway rate was created but for the most part the roads remained as bad as ever, it being usual to throw a few large stones in the ruts and even that was not always done. People were resigned to this sort of thing as they had never known anything better. One country squire despairing of improvement measured the width of his native ruts and had his carriage designed accordingly.

If a neighbourhood was very bad travellers avoided it so that in some parts even a cart was a rarity.

As the century advanced the authorities began to consider the question of turnpikes. In the days before universal rating the idea was not a bad one as everyone who travelled other than foot passengers paid for the roads. These turnpikes were set up all over the country. High white gates every five miles or so and minute turnpike houses of which many survive today. From them the keeper ran out whenever he heard the sound of horses or wheels on the road. At night the wretched man might be roused several times by knocks on the door or windows. No wonder they became bad tempered and morose and inclined to charge more than they should. The rider on horseback paid $1\frac{1}{2}$d at each tollgate, a cart or carriage with one horse $4\frac{1}{2}$d and a pair in hand 1/6. Cattle sheep and pigs were paid for at so much a score. A list of tolls was displayed at each tollhouse but as many could not read the keeper often charged what he pleased.

The turnpikes were very unpopular; to stop every few miles and pay out good money was extremely irksome and the roads did not seem to be much improved.

Signposts were very few and in many parts non existent. It was often necessary to have a guide on the journey; it is a fact that a man coming from Ringwood to Lymington alone lost his way completely and a guide was essential on even a short journey.

Beside the roads there were the tracks over the country by which the pack horses went. Merchants loaded their horses at Lymington fair and set off over the pack horse roads to sell their wares in the country towns and villages. As many as 30 or 40 horses would proceed in a string, the leader wearing a bell to warn other pack owners of their approach through the narrow lanes with their high banks. In some parts of the country these tracks were the only way of getting about and everything was carried by horses in panniers or sometimes on a narrow sledge.

INNS

A traveller usually had a choice but must select with care. There were firstly the grand establishments, the posting houses which catered for the quality travellers who posted in their own carriages or postchaises. They might accommodate a riding gentleman if he was accompanied by a servant and some accepted passengers from the mail coach–some did not but they never stooped so low as to take a passenger from the common stage.

These people had to go to the inns which catered for them but they had the satisfaction of knowing there were others of a still inferior order. The passenger in the waggon and the walker on foot were seldom admitted or if they were they were pushed into the kitchens and fed on the remains.

The last class, the waggon passengers and wayfarers, were catered for by the "hedge" inns who charged 9d or 1/- for bed and supper.

CHAPTER EIGHT

The Local Emigrants

On the breaking-out of the war with Revolutionary France, our town had an accession of new visitors: the Royalist refugees, of both sexes, who fled before the Republican Terror. They were nearly all of gentle birth—many of them noble by rank and title. These, in their turn, were soon followed by a larger number—officers and civilians, who had embraced the royalist cause, and escaped the massacres and proscriptions which everywhere menaced them. The unfortunates landed everywhere on the south-west coast, without any means of support; and were hospitably received, in pity to their sufferings. Their numbers continually increased; and at last the English government, in order to provide them with the means of living, collected them into several corps, with a view to utilizing their services in the war that was then carried on in Flanders and the northern frontier of France, under the Duke of York, or in an expedition intended to make a diversion in his favour, on the coasts of La Vendee and Brittany. Nine regiments were nominally formed, but only three were fully filled: the remaining being mere *cadres*, to be developed as opportunity offered. In order to be near the coast, they were collected here; just as had been the case at earlier periods; for our position has always made us rather prominent during Continental wars.

One of these French corps was of considerable note: and was the earliest formed. It had already seen hot service on the French frontier; and was, at first, known as *La Chatre's*, from its commander; but afterwards, both here and on the Continent, as *The Loyal Emigrants*. In the actions in Flanders it had been reduced to about four hundred men—all tried, trusty, and brave: lives too valuable to be lightly wasted; but preserved for important occasions. They were, in fact, a body of officers, merely keeping together in ranks for the sake of their support. They were the salt wherewith the raw Breton peasants were to be savoured, when collected in insurrection. These gentlemen (for so we may term them) occupied different buildings at various tradesmen's houses, where they were both liked and respected.

Another corps was a body of Marines; formed out of the sailors and officers of the French Naval (Royalist) Service, and known as the "Royal Marine." They were commanded by

Count d'Hector, and numbered about 600 men. Their quarters were to the north of the town, at Buckland.

The third corps was known as the French Artillery; and was formed principally from the gunners who had defended Toulon against the Republicans; and who, with such of the inhabitants as could escape, had taken refuge on board the English Fleet under Admiral Hood. They were commanded by Col. Rothalier: numbered about 400; and occupied the (now) Malt-house in New Lane, with some houses and a long row of stables and buildings (since destroyed), on the western side, just opposite.

There were also two or three other regiments, or parts of regiments, of which we can give no particular detail. One was known as Muiron's: another as Willot's; the remainder were named from their respective commanders, Count De Puisaye, Count D'Hervilly, Col. De Mortemar, and Col. Dresnay. They were quartered in different places—about the Quay—at a barn near the present Station Street—and in other similar localities. In the while, the different corps reached about three thousand men. To these we may add, as part of the Foreign element, a number of their friends—royalist refugees, who had taken refuge at Toulon from the southern central districts of France. They were a motley group of men, women, and children.

Accumulating by degrees, a time at length arrived for action. The plans of the French Royalists on the Continent embraced an invasion from the Prussian frontier; and the Prince de Conde, on the Rhine, and the Duke of York, on the side of Holland, were both ready.

A descent from England on the coast of Brittany was projected in 1795, so as to create a diversion in their favour; and accordingly a fleet assembled off Lymington, in Yarmouth Roads, in the June of that year, under the command of Sir John Borlase Warren. It contained the complete outfit and all munitions of war, for an army to be raised in Brittany. Fifty sail of transports accompanied it; which took in the troops we have mentioned. The whole sailed, and joined the fleet, off Ushant, commanded by Lord Bridport; and thence steered direct for Belle Isle and Quiberon Bay. A second squadron was to call at the Channel Islands, and take in similar troops collected there, who were to form a subsidiary diversion by way of St. Malo; and the Duc d'Artois (afterwards Charles X) and the Duc de Bourbon, were to join the army on reaching France.

A naval victory off L'Orient (1795) cleared the way for a landing in Quiberon Bay; but the events which followed are beyond our limited sphere, and are more matter for history. The failure of the expedition may be read in many works, to which the curious can turn. Our business is with our Lymington residents. The most fortunate died sword in hand, after exhibiting the greatest bravery; others, despairing, turned their weapons against themselves; a few were saved, through the waves, by the English boats, and conveyed to the ships. All the rest—the officers, and about forty or fifty gentlemen of rank who had accompanied the ill-starred expedition—were shot.

The original plan had been to land on the coast, and make a junction on the right with the Chouan chiefs in La Vendee; then, with the united forces, to march on Paris; while the Royalist chiefs on the Rhine did the same from an opposite direction. Tinteniac, and Georges Cadoudal, had swept round the coasts of Lower Brittany, and were at the rendezvous; but, as in all undisciplined bands, jealousies led to disputes and to divergence of action. Yet on the first landing all seemed well. One of *our* corps (for we may call them on the present occasion) under Count d'Hervilly, surprised Fort Penthièvre, which commands the bay and peninsula; but it was again taken by the Republicans. D'Hervilly was fortunate enough to be mortally wounded, and so spared the sight of the fatal reverse that quickly followed. The division of the Count de Sombreuil was driven back from the fort into the Quiberon peninsula.

The first effort of the attack had failed; but M. de Puisaye, the leader of the expedition, wished to make another attempt, supported by the ships and gunboats, to resist the republican column that was approaching. Admiral Warren did all he could; but the sea was stormy and rough; and the unfortunate emigrants, pressed between the bayonets of their enemies, and the waves behind them, were lost. Hundreds were drowned or slaughtered on shore; numbers of the officers threw themselves on their swords; and the unfortunate remnant, trusting to offers (as they said) of quarter, surrendered themselves prisoners. The royalist corps had lost more than 1200 men, and 102 officers; and about 1300 were saved in the English boats and taken on board the fleet.

The survivors of the fatal combat were carried off to Vannes, a neighbouring town, where a military commission at once condemned them to death. The Chasseurs of the 19th demi-brigade (French)—with the generous instinct of soldiers—refused to execute the order; both officers and men joining in the determination. A battalion of Volunteers of Paris (as they were termed) comprised of the populace order; and MM. de Somberuil, de Broglie, de la Landelle, and Mgr. de Hercé, the (last) bishop of Dol, with other gentlemen (twenty two in all), were shot forthwith, on a neighbouring road or promenade known as The Garenne. The others, about 160 in number, were taken to Auray, a town a few miles distant, where they too were shot on the plain by the bay. The place where they fell is still known as the Pointe des Emigres. Many a brave gentleman, who once walked our street, died there.

From 1795, till the Restoration in 1815, their remains lay unnoticed in their common grave; but at that period they were collected by the Royalist party into a more honorable sepulchre, and two monuments were raised to their memory. One is a sepulchral edifice or mausoleum, in which are sculptured the names of all who fell (952 in number), with inscriptions and texts suitable to the feelings of their party; and also busts of their leaders. The other, at a short distance, is a "chapelle expiatoire" (a religious chapel), with a column of granite surmounted by a cross.

The first act of the drama was over; and Lymington was emptied of its foreign guests for a time. The successes of Hoche, the destruction of La Vendee, and the rise of Bonaparte, prevented such an attempt being repeated. But as our town still retained its convenient position on the Channel Coast, the gap was at once filled up; and it was fixed on as a military depot for a miscellaneous body of soldiers, the debris of various armies and troops that had fought on the Continent, particularly in Holland and the North of France. They were a more miscellaneous and rough assemblage of men—common soldiers only.

Their behaviour was as their position in life: they were a turbulent and unruly set of men. Duels among the officers were not infrequent; crimes of violence (among the men) were but little thought of: they had long been accustomed to warfare and scenes of blood.

Flogging was continually going on at the barrack yard in Church Lane: six or more of a morning was a common and ordinary occurrence. Two rival bodies once turned out (as I have been informed) with fixed bayonets, in Broad Lane, where the parades were held: the drummers on each side, with their drums, ready to beat the charge. Bloodshed would have ensued, had not the officers rushed between the men, and stopped them by bodily interference. Several murders were committed: one was just opposite the parade ground: suicides were frequent. The sailors, from the gunboats and cutters in the Solent, were the causes of frequent tumult and riots.

For the sake of distinction we may call these Germans, though various nationalities were represented among them. They were generally quartered where the others had been lodged:— the Dutch Artillery, in New Lane; and the others in the different barrack-buildings. The old Tithing Barn served as a general hospital. They must have been packed closely together in a way that would astonish our modern refinement. Sickness and mortality among them were great; and their hardships were severe; but who could think of such trifles in the midst of the confusion reigning over all Europe.

These German troops were never (at once) removed; although changes continually took place, by departures and fresh arrivals. They stayed here till the Peace of Amiens, when all was at an end. Prisoners were then exchanged; and foreigners sent home: except those who had settled in the town.

Besides these regular troops, large bodies of Militia were constantly moving about during the summer months, all through the southern counties. We were visited every year by bodies of men (in the whole about 1000 or 1200 at a time)—Militia or Fencibles, who were quartered in the numerous public-houses, or encamped on Pennington Common, and such localities.

Every person who considered himself respectable, from the lower to the higher ranks, was thoroughly loyal. Accordingly, every 4th of June, on the King's birthday, there was a great demonstration. The regular troops, the militia, and the local corps, lined the High Street, from the Church to the Town Hall and fired a volley; while the artillery responded from the Parade Ground in Church Lane; and the bells rung.

Our local corps raised here, were a Pike Corps, with white uniforms; and a small body of Artillery, about which a story was long current. In the first hurry of its formation, cannon could not be procured; and some enthusiast, burning with patriotic ardour, suggested that a leaden pump-barrel should be rigged out as a cannon, so as to enable the men to practice serving the gun, ramming, etc. The idea was not bad: but there was too much of the ludicrous in the proposal. The appellation of "The Pump Corps" could not be got rid of, till the corps was finally dissolved at the peace in 1814; when the Depot was broken up altogether.

At the time of the Boulogne flotilla, in 1802, when invasion was expected, all the waggons at the neighbouring farms were registered and numbered, so as to carry off the non-combatant population into the Forest, in case of the enemy's landing.

Besides Lymington, other neighbouring towns had their emigrant visitors. The Duc de Bourbon (father of the Duc d'Enghien) resided at Newport; and there formed acquaintance with Sophy Daw, a fisherman's daughter, who was destined to influence his future life; and to be involved in his historic and mysterious end. She (as the Baroness de Feucheres) died at Bure Homage, near Christchurch, in 1836. Her father-confessor, the Rev. J. Stapleton, after her death, lived here; and lies in our churchyard (*d.* 1839).

All departed (many, perhaps, to fight and fall at Waterloo, either for or against us), except some who had married or settled here—perhaps having deserted from their former ranks, and unwilling to run the risk of being recognized. Quiet stillness reigned again; but tales about the Frenchmen, and the Dutchmen, as they were termed, were numerous and current till late years, among the older inhabitants, many of whom had learnt some colloquial conversation-phrases from the necessary intercourse with the strangers during the lapse of twenty years.

There were no regular barracks built in the town; but the various corps were quartered in these among other localities:

1. The last house in Church Lane on the west, and the garden where the serpentine wall is, was the general Depot and Parade Ground; more extended than at present; and no trees around it.

2. A row of barrack houses on the Quay facing the Masonic Hall, which was then a private residence where the Colonel lived. (In 1813, Le Chevalier Baron de Macquard).

3. The old Farm-house at Buckland, to the south of Mrs. Southey's residence. The farm buildings thereto attached.

4. The Tithe Barn—used as a hospital. Two tenements (now Mogshed Cottages) nearly opposite.

5. In New Lane, the Malt-house and a long row of buildings on the opposite side of the road. (These were for the Artillery).

6. A large barn just beyond Station Street (now destroyed).

7. A long row of buildings on the west side of *The Angel* yard: others at *The Anchor and Hope*, as also at all the different inns in the town.

Broad Lane was the general parade ground. The wide green spaces, from which it derived its name, have been since enclosed.

The following Regiments, English and Foreign, were quartered in Lymington, or encamped in the vicinity of the town, at the respective dates given—

1756—A Hessian Corps.

1780.

N. Devon Militia. S. Hants Militia. S. Lincoln Militia. Surrey Militia.

The old Tithe Barn built *c*.1250. It served as a hospital for French royalists evacuated from the continent in 1795 after a disastrous military campaign against the Republicans culminating in their final defeat at Quiberon bay.

1781—The 1st Royals.

1784.
1st Dragoon Guards. The Prince of Wales' Regiment.

1792.
42nd Foot. 3rd Foot. 2nd (or Queen's). 19th Regiment. 92nd Regiment. South Hants Militia. Monmouth Militia.

1794—1798.
119th Regiment. 90th Foot. 10th Foot. Cheshire Militia. Monmouth Militia. Berks Militia. 2nd (or Queen's). Loyal Emigrants. Toulonnese Artillery. Dutch Rifles. Dutch Artillery. King's German Legion.

1800—1814.
A Hessian Corps. 1st Royals. Queen's Bays. 31st Foot. N. Devon Militia. S. Hants Militia. S. Lincoln Militia. Surrey Militia.

CHAPTER NINE

The Church

The Parish Church is the only building in Lymington that can lay any real claim to antiquity. Parts of the present structure date back to about 1250, but there is evidence that a Lymington Chapel existed long before this date. The present Church is dedicated to St. Thomas the Apostle.

The building was originally an exact Latin cross, to which in about 1325 a Mortuary Chapel was added by the Courtenays in the North-Eastern corner. Here, under an immense grey slab, originally inlaid with a brass figure and armorial shields at the corners, are laid the remains of some of the branches of the Courtenay stock, but their names are unknown, the brasses having been stripped away. Till the end of the 18th century this chapel was separated from the church by a carved oak railing: then it was thrown into the general area of the building. Time, neglect and wanton devastation have wrought their effects on the church as on the town itself. It was gutted during the civil wars, when the Puritan soldiers occupied it, and erected some kind of fortification or block house at the eastern end, in the churchyard, to command the town. In 1662, on the Restoration, the place was in a sad state, the fences destroyed, the fabric desecrated and everything in a ruinous condition. The inhabitants however set to work, repaired the damages in the style of their time, and built the tower, pulling down the south transept for that purpose. A clock was set up in the tower in 1674, which was replaced in 1835 and a peal of six bells was completed in 1684. The Church was enlarged several times from 1756 onwards. In 1911 there was a general restoration rendered possible by a legacy from Mrs. Earley, who also left her two houses (117 and 118 High Street) to the town for Municipal Offices. In 1927 the Courtenay Mortuary Chapel was restored, and re-dedicated by the Bishop of Winchester. It is interesting to note that at one time Henry Francis Lyte, the author of the hymn "Abide with Me" held the curacy at Lymington.

In presenting the following accounts it will be noticed that many items appear to be outside the jurisdiction of the Church, but it should be remembered that in those days the Corporation was not a rating authority, the towns only income being the few tolls from the quay and half yearly fairs together with a few small properties. The Church therefore paid for nearly everything, the Churchwarden issuing demands for rates as and when required—sometimes as many as twenty times in a year. As assessments were low (the highest being £40 for a larger house) and the rate perhaps as low as 4d, this was not an undue burden (except to the poor) but to see the collector twenty times in a year must have been the source of extreme irritation.

THE VESTRY ACCOUNTS BEGINNING 1669

Churchwardens' Regulations— 16th Century

The Toppings of the trees in the Churchyard belong to the Vicar of the Parish. Statute 35 EDW 1.

None sit in Church with their Hats on – and that none contend or quarrel about Place or upon any other occasion, make any Broil or Brawling there.

And that none depart out of the Church unless in Case of Necessity till the Service be fully ended.

They shall also chastise the boys who are rude and disorderly. Fines are 1/– for absenting from Church, 1/– for not abiding there till service and sermon ended, 1/– for not behaving orderly and soberly while there, and notwithstanding they have paid the said Mulct they must also be presented at the next Visitation.

If any Carter, Wainman, Carman, Drover, Horse-courser, Waggoner, Butcher, Higler travel in the Lord's Day £1. If travel by Boat, Whery, Barge or Lighter 5/–. If any meet for Bullbaitings, Bearbaitings, Interludes, Common plays or other sport 3/4, and where no distress is to be had, the offenders to be put in the stocks. They should also frequently to visit on the Lords Day alehouses and taverns, both in time of Divine Service and out of it, any tippling 3/4 and Master of the House 10/– and 5/– more for using his trade on the Lord's Day. To levy a penalty of 1/– or 2/– on those who profanely curse and swear to be levied by Distress, if none, to be set in the stocks or if under sixteen, whipped. Shoemakers putting Boots and Shoes on sale on a Sunday, 3/4 *and the goods*.

If one is assaulted and beaten in a Church, it is not lawful to return or give back any blows.

Penalty for striking another in Church or Churchyard – excommunication. But if with a weapon, the offender to lose one of his Ears.

Each parish to keep a large Engine, a hand engine and a leather pipe on penalty of £8.

The first person to bring in an Engine to a fire, shall be paid £1 10s. 0d. as an Encouragement.

The person bringing the second Engine £1, the third 10/–.

This was the reign of Charles 2nd who was crowned in 1661, eight years before our Vestry Book commenced.

In 1662 the Act of Uniformity had been passed enforcing the use of the Prayer Book in all Churches and a great many Ministers who refused to conform resigned their livings.

The Great Plague had broken out in London in 1665 and had spread into the country districts in that and the following year for we read in our Borough books for 1665:–

"For fourteen days and nights watching in dangerous times, when the sickness was in other places" 6s.

and again in 1666:–

"For conducting Elizabeth Bunch to Ringwood in the time of the visitation" 1/–.

That is the background of the time of which I now refer 1669. The accounts for that year are headed "The Account of Richard Eden and John Burrard Gent, Churchwardens of the parish of Lymington for the year last past 1669."

The Incumbent was Samuel Torksey.

RECEIPTS	£	s.	d.
For upon two rates at £ 4 3s. 8d. ye rate	8	7	4
For breaking the ground in the Church for Mr. Pryanlse		6	8
Of Tiplers in the time of Divine Service		2	0
Of Mr. Scott for breaking the ground in the Church		6	8
	£ 9	2	8

Note 100 years after viz: 1769 the rate was for two of £14 10s. 0d.

Wages in   1620 wage was 4½d. per day.
            1632 wage was 6d. per day.
            1680 wage was 8d. per day.
            Background—Plague 1665.

	£	s.	d.
Boro Books of fourteen days watching in dangerous times when the sickness was in other places		6	0
1666 Elizabeth Blunch to R in the time of the visitation		1	0
Church Books begin 1669. 8th year of Charles II.			
Two Church Rates of	4	3	8
Burial in Church		6	8
Wine for two Communions		6	0
Wagon per day			8
1670 South Transept—South Wall of Chancel rebuilt to archading in south side of sanctury.			
Cost of Tower	413	19	4
Eight rates of	64	3	3
1671 twenty Rates of	4	4	4

Two year Penticost Money: 74 houses 3 1
Primitive Agriculture: Badger 1/–, Hedgehog 4d, Otter 2/6, Bullfinch ½d. Sparrows 2d doz.
Chaffinch ½d. Stoat 4d. Weasel 2d. Fox 1/–.
1685 Highways 2 10 4
Puritan Names: Obediah Newell, Wilderness Watson, Hercules Hunter, Abigail Sheppard,
Hizikiah Hinks, Phineas Wright.
To Ringers in Beer when the Bishop came to town 7 8

DISBURSEMENTS

	£	s.	d.
Paid Mr. Harmood due of the foot of his account	1	11	0
Gave by myself to Travellers		12	7
To the Churchwardens of Boldre		10	6
Spent at the Visitations	1	13	9
5 qrts. of Lime to John Bale		15	0
To Mr. Wale for mending the windows as ye Bill	1	9	9
To him for a fox's head		1	0
To Thomas Badcock to make the Lime into Mortor		3	0
For building Mr. Scott's seate		5	0
To James Rossiter for a fox's head		1	0
To Giles Wing for two loads of sand		2	0
To him for fetching a load of Lime		2	0
For a warrant for Edward Elines			6
To Mr. Sampson that he gave to Travellers		15	6
To him for a Warrant for Dods			6
And that he laid out for weigh of loads			4
To John Blake for "frework"		1	2
To Mark Hurst for hanging the Bell		2	0
For hanging the Churchyard gates		1	0
To Tom Tiller as ye Bill		6	6
Allowed Mr. Urry two rates		1	0
To Good Musson two rates			6
To Mish Quint for Williams his house two rates			6
For wine for the two Communions		6	0
	9	3	1
Receipts	9	2	8

Due from the Pish to the said Churchwardens   5
     Allowed Easter 1672
     Signed by seven Burgesses.

The next year 1670 we see the collection of subscriptions together with the sale of old timber and lead for the pulling down of the South Transept and the building of the present tower in its place. At the same time the South Wall of the Chancel was rebuilt as far as the arcading in the south side of the sanctuary.

The total income from all sources for this year including eight rates at £4 3s. 3d. was £420 4s. 8d. of which the sum of £389 5s. 4d. was paid to Mr. Mitchell the builder and a small balance of £24 14s. 0d. being paid in the following year.

OTHER ITEMS

The next year no less than twenty rates at £4 4s. 4d. per rate were made.

1671. Incumbent Samuel Watson.

1673. For ringing the great Bell once   1   0
     (The Great Bell was rung only for notable persons buried in Church).

John Dore for carriage of 4,000 slatts and sand to the Church   4   2

For care of Vagabond persons to Pennington   1   0

For six ditto quarters for one night   1   6

VAGABONDS

Tending to show the unsettled condition of the country as a whole and of the poverty in and around the town. Vagabonds are described as being:–

1.   All persons gathering alms under pretence.

2.   All going about as Collectors.

3.   All Fencers and Bearwards, common players of Interludes and persons who for gain, cause to act Tragedy, Comedy, Opera or Play.

4.   All Minstrals, Juglers and persons pretending to be Egyptians and Fortunetellers or like crafty science.

5.   Persons who run away and leave the wives and children.

6.   Petty Chapmen and Pedlers not being licenced.

7.   All persons wandering abroad and lodging in Alehouses, Barns, Outhouses and in the open air.

The above are described as a constant supply to the Gallows and for transportation to our American colonies.

	£	s	d
To Edis Balton for the Diall Board		17	0
Will Broadshaw for half a days work			10

(1674. Broadshaw was a builder by trade and lived at 122 High Street.)

	£	s	d
John Ashley for a Bellrope..		1	8

John Ashley lived at the corner of Ashley Lane (now Rands) and was a leatherworker by trade, he made collars for the bull-baitings in the fields at the bottom of this lane.

1674

	£	s	d
For horsehire for the Visitation		8	0
Mr. Wise for setting up the clock	2	10	0
For Charcole			8
1675. 800 feet of paving stone	3	0	0
For bottoming the pulpit cushion and fringe		1	0
To the ringers at Christmas		1	6
Washing the Church linen		4	6
1676. Old lead sold for 12/– cwt.		12	0
Two years Pentecost money		3	1
To Parker for mending the Churchyard doors and the lock and bolt of the Great Church door		2	0
A new Table Cloth for the Communion Table		18	0
A new Chest		9	6
Three loads of Lime	2	10	0
Spent at the Petty Sessions		1	6
Gave the men a drink to help set up the Kings Arms		2	0
Goody Lyne for washing the Linnen		1	6
Martha Hills for wash and skow the flagons etc.		1	6
Eight Polcatts Heads			8
One Foxhead		1	0

VERMIN

By custom the churchwardens of all parishes were authorised to pay the following prices for heads:–

Badgers 1s. 0d.	Hedgehog 4d.	Otter 2s. 6d.
Bullfinch ½d.	Sparrow (doz.) 2d.	Chaffinch ½d.
Stoat 4d.	Weasil 2d.	Fox 1s. 0d.
Polecat 4d.		

	£	s	d
Horsehire to Broken and Lyndhurst		1	6
1677. A seat in the South Isle		5	0
A tun of stones		8	4
To poor seamen, castaway and taken by the French	1	0	5

	£	s	d
Wm. Hedgman for the Railes in the Chansel and for the Ironwork	2	0	0
For 12 Matts		5	0
John Hills for cleansing the Pewter etc.		3	6
Gave to sixteen poor Dutchmen		5	4
For the Book of Homilies		11	0
Rob Cleeves for keeping the Clock and ring Bell	2	10	0
A Brush to cleanse the Church		1	6
Olye for the Bells			6
Ringers on Gunpowder Treason Day		2	0
Wyer for the Clock			4
For Trophy Money	1	7	0
Making the Royal Aid rates		4	0
Thomas Elliott for keeping a Vagabond and having him to the Justice		12	0
Rich Hurst for mending the Bell Wheele			6
1680. For Nailes for the Church		1	0
Bell ropes		7	0
Poor Seamen out of Algiers at several times	2	4	4

OUT OF ALGIERS

These were captives taken by Algerian pirates, who were now so daring as to infest the English coasts, revenging the attacks of Blake during the Commonwealth.

	£	s	d
1 lb. of Candles			5
For a Watch		2	0
18 tuns of healing stones at 6s. 0d. per tun			
Allowed Mark Hurst six rates			6
1681. John Hills (Parish Clarke) wages per annum	2	10	0
Wm. Morris thirty seven days for work and ½d. = 1s. 2d. per day	2	3	9
Henry Wale for colouring the Pulpitt		2	6
1683. Joseph Layton – Minister.			
1684. Twenty three Rates at £4 9s. 2½d.			
1685. For ye order to change ye King's name in ye Prayers		1	0
Expended by order of the pish on ye Highways	2	10	4
Overseers of the Highway appointed every year.			
For mending a place in ye roof		3	6
For cleansing the Church and way from the snow		4	6
For trussing the Tenor		2	6
A new bier		8	6

The poor were buried without a coffin and a bier was used to convey the body to the grave. This bier had to be kept at the parish expense.

	£	s	d
Allowed eighteen rates to John Blake at 16d. a rate, for a poor child he keeps	1	4	0
Paid Widow Hills for expenses when Dr. Crow was taken up by the Officers ..		16	0
For expenses in going to Totton with Dr. Crow		1	6
For horsehire at the same time		2	0
Paid Henry Gookey, William Edwards and Edward Brent for amending the Kings Highways	4	2	5
Paid the Apporator for two books and a Proclamacon about the fast		2	0
To three poor soldiers		1	6
For the amending the Highways	2	2	0

Wilderness Watson, a collector of rates.

1690 John Darby – Minister.

1692. Easter Tuesday.

It is the day ordered at a Publique meeting of this parish that no person shall for the future receive or have relief from this parish, but such as shall publiquely weare on their right arme the letters P and L which the Collectors are desired to see done before they relieve them.

> Robt Smyth
> Eho. Bulkly.

1693. John Hinton – Minister.

1693. At a General Meeting of the pish it is ordered that the Churchwardens for the time being do sue all persons to an Excommunication, that do refuse to pay their privy Tithes and rates to the Church at the cost and charges of the parish.

	£	s	d
Paid to Widow Fry for keeping of a boy that was wounded when the Troopers came hither		10	0
For amending the Church Walls		1	4
Mrs. How for amending of the surplus			8
Mr. Reade for a Hearsecloth	4	0	0
Pd Geo Clarke for whipping a vagabond		1	0

Beggars were first whipped, then given food and refreshment after which they were escorted to the bounds of the parish and given a pass to their destination which asked neighbouring officers to send them on and treat them kindly. The regulation was that they must go directly to the town required and not deviate from the route on the way.

	£	s	d
1694. Paid for Horsehire to send away Seamen that had the smallpox to Ringwood		3	0
Mr. Riggs for Bread and Beere for the prisoners which came from France ..		4	10
William Hodgman for making three frames for ye Ten Commandments ..		4	10
To Widdow Thorne for Lodging of poore seamen, quartered upon her by the Constables		4	0½
Henry Waleson for glazing the windows and writing the Ten Commandments	4	2	0½

1695. To the ringers when the plot was discovered   10   0
     This was the Assassination Plot and was the conspiracy to attack and kill King William at Richmond.

1696. Benjamin Brougham – Minister.

	£	s	d
1696. For five pairs of Indentures for parish children	1	0	0
To Mr. Waleson for glazing and painting the steeple	3	6	4
1697. Pd for Napkins for the Communion	1	6	0
For Tarr for tarring the Ladders		4	0
For a stock lock		1	0
Two dozen Leather Bucketts	4	0	0
Thomas Shepherd of *Woodside* his rates			6
Mr. Wale for 2,000 of Tyles at 1s. 6d. a 100	1	11	0
John King for half tun of Timber		15	0
More for timber		19	0
For sawing of timber		4	6
Two Bushells of Tilepins		5	0
John Blake for Firehooks and Chains wt 9 score and 12 pounds	4	16	0
For one Cross Tyle		2	6

1700. Thomas Warre for mending the stocks etc.

1701. Henry Hackman paid a fine of £1 4s. 0d. on taking over the seat of Mrs. Priaulx in the Church. (From this date payment for seats became common).

1702. It was agreed at a parish meeting that the Church and Chancel shall be sealed, parged and plastered in a workmanlike manner at the charges of the said parish.

1703. Paid for Charcole   10
     We whose hands are hereunto subscribed do impower the Overseers of the Poor for the year to agree with such persons as keeps the parish children for to Cloath them and furnish them with all other necessaries as they shall think fit.

1705. Wm Newman for the vain   2   0

1706. We the parishioners and other inhabitants of the parish of Lymington whose names are under written, having made choice of Benjamin Wood, Master of Arts of Queens College, Oxon for our Minister of Lymington and agreed to allow him out of our own free gift, certain sums of money to be paid half yearly towards his maintenance, do hereby declare our great satisfaction in the choice we so made of Mr. Wood to be our Minister and our willingness to continue to him the several sums agreed to by the respective inhabitants of our parish afore- said in the same manner as formerly so long as he shall be our Minister. And as a further testi- mony of our gratitude for his diligence and faithfulness in the discharge of his function among us we do hereby promise to pay to the said Mr. Wood the one half of the sums agreed to as aforesaid in such way and method as we have hitherto paid the whole, so long as he shall continue out of place in case any attempt is made by any one to displace him.

	£	s	d
1706. Moneys paid to Council at Winton at the last Assizes	3	4	6
To the serjants man		2	6
Wm. Squibb for his pains and horsehire to Winton		10	0
Expenses and horsehire at the sametime	2	1	6
To James Baker expenses when Sir Robert Smythe and several of the parish were there about the Law		16	3
Mr. Hackman for 200 of Tiles		3	4
(Today £5.)			
Wm. Rossiter for a load of Clay and carridge		2	0
Mr. Stacey for 500 of Laths		6	0
(Today £8 6s. 8d.)			
Daniel Elliott for Bell Roapes		4	0

1707. Lymington May 20th.

At a Parish Meeting held at Mrs. Wrights at *The Bugle* in Lymington this day and year above written. It was unanimously agreed upon as follows viz:

Whereas the Parish of Lymington by their own voluntary subscriptions together with the privy tithes and perquisites of the said Parish (which have always been allowed by the Vicars of Boldre for the time being) have always maintained their Ministers here. And whereas for this among other reasons the said Parish have always chosen their Minister, no Vicar of Boldre ever interposing in that affair. And whereas the Rev. Mr. John Howel present Vicar of Boldre contrary to his oath of perpetual residence upon his Vicarage, and in opposition to the choice of the said parish pretends to settle himself in the said Parish of Lymington, we the Churchwardens, Parishioners and other Inhabitants of the said Parish of Lymington do hereby declare that we do utterly disapprove of these unprecedented proceedings of the aforesaid Vicar, and that we will endeavour by all due Methods of Law to oblige the said Vicar of Boldre to recede from these his unreasonable pretentions, and to reside as in duty bound upon his said Vicarage.

And that this our Agreement and Declaration may not fail of its desired effect, we do furthermore consent and agree and hereby authorise and appoint, our Trusty and Well beloved friend Mr. Charles Hackman (our true and Lawfull Attorney) to prosecute the Law against the aforesaid Mr. John Howel, in such manner as is or shall hereafter be agreed upon and as we shall be advised for the purpose above mentioned. In witness whereof, we have hereunto set our hands the day and year above written.

Thirty seven signatures.

	£	s	d
1707. To the french prisoners		4	6
Hedgehog heads		1	10
Expenses at several times in the parish business		12	3

1708. Henry Hackman and Wilderness Watson, surveyors of the Highway. The last time the election to this office appears in the Vestry records.

	£	s	d
To money to the Ringers when the news came of the Duke of Marlborough taking Owdinard		7	0
To the Ringers in bere when the Bishop came to town		7	8
ditto when we obtained the victory over the French		5	6
1710. A messenger to Andover for Mr. Horncock		8	0
To a poor seaman by order		1	0
To Mr. Walton for preaching	1	1	6

1711. Thomas Jenner – Minister.

It was decided at a Parish Meeting that no Churchwarden should be allowed more than £1 10s. 0d. expenses at a visitation and if he exceeds this amount it will be paid out of his own pocket.

	£	s	d
1713. To the Churchwardens of Boldre		10	0
(note 6d. less to 1729/30).			
Five pints of Oyle for the bells		5	0
Oyle and Cullers for the window shutters		2	9
Expenses at *The Nag's Head* on parish business		2	1
A pound of candles			6
1714. 9 Foxheads and Graysheads		9	0
Mending five leather Bushels		1	6
Six mats for the Church		5	0
John Hurst, his Clerks and Sextons wages	5	0	0
1716. To the Ringers more upon the success at Preston and Scotland over the Rebels at two several times		17	0
1717. Samuel Serle for twenty seven tuns of Wallstones	2	0	6
Freight and charges of Landing them	1	7	0
Wharfidge of them		4	6
Workmen in beere about the Wall		1	8
For a New Surplus	3	0	0
John Cleves for painting the Kings Arms	1	10	0
Beere for Ringers for Victory in Scotland		11	0
To a poor old man		1	0
To the woman that came from Shoram		2	6

	£	s	d
John Hurst for digging two graves for poor people		1	4
Two stotes heads			4

1718. Franklyn Powell – Minister.

	£	s	d
1718. To 105 feet of stones for coping of the Churchyard Walls	5	5	0
Freight Wharfage and carriage		17	4
To workmen about the churchyard wall and other Materials	1	14	6
A brush, flagg stafe and nailes		3	4½
Three Sacrament Days for wine	1	7	0
4½ yards Black broad cloth at 11/– yard	2	9	6
12 yards Fine White Sarsnett at 3s. 0d. yard	1	16	0
(A very fine light weight silk, very bright).			
For cutting, making and bringing		7	6
For six silk tasells about 14 ozs.	1	6	0
To work done by Sam Miller about ye Cupilor		4	0
1719. To Mr. Watson for Trees	2	12	4
Carridge of Trees and digging holes		8	6
1720. Thirty Rates at £5 3s. 7d.	155	7	6
Plus four rates at £5 3s. 10d.	20	15	4
(Alterations to the Church).			
Mr. Burrards rates for the parsonage, which he refuses to pay	3	15	0
(Paid the following year).			
1721. Cash received of Mr. Charles Bulkley for 600 bricks		7	0
Rates not collected :–			
Late Stephen Pitt for Miorymead		1	8
To Samuel Bright one days work		1	2
Jas Redstone one days work		1	8
Robert Ellots for work on the Litton wall		5	10
For work on the Engon house		19	10
For altering the pulpit cloath		1	0
To Mr. Knapton for Painting ye Canopy to the Pulpitt	1	11	6

1722. Parishioners name entered in books
>   Hercules Hinton
>   Phineas Wright
>   Calob Sheppard

	£	s	d
By Exp: when being chosen, being Easter Tuesday		6	6
Cleansing the Mallies and other weeds out of the Church	1	0	1
To Crow and Sheppard for repairing the Engeon		8	0

	£	s	d
To Beer when the Engeon was played		2	6

The Engeon to which frequent reference is made was a hand pump for putting out fires in the town. It was housed in the churchyard near the West Door.

	£	s	d
To the Fordingbridge singers	1	1	0

1723. This was an early attempt to regulate the music of the choirs, throughout the Country.

	£	s	d
James Curle for filling the Engeon with water		1	0
To the singing Master for learning poor Boyes	1	0	0
1725. Seven poor slaves from Algiers		4	0
1726. Mr. Vessey died		6	8
To a labourer for clearing the Churchyard		1	6
To the Minister in Mr. Powells absense		7	6
John Bull for four Hedgehogs			8
1727. For a paper book			3
His Majesty's Coronation, to ye Ringers at Jenck's and two legs of Mutton ..		13	3

Coronation of George II.
Parishioners Obediah Newell
        George Gold.

1728. Richard Fishlake – Minister.

	£	s	d
1730. Exp: at Winton at Visitation	1	1	2
Exp. one night at Redbridge and Hursley		10	6
Two Horsehires to Winton		8	0
Exp. at Mrs. Riggs when rec'd the Book		5	0
Mrs. Riggs for 3 quarts of Communion Wine		9	0

1730. Jacob Marks (Landlord of Yeoman Inn)

	£	s	d
For three Brushes		10	0
For making a surplice		10	0
Beer for men to play Engin		2	0
Mending the Engin House	1	19	7
Whitewashing the Church		7	8
Gave to Castaway Seamen		2	0
Paid Dick the Painter for Painting	2	5	0

1726   Rates not Collected:–

		s	d
Wid Miller 12 at 1d.		1	0
Sarah Davis 12 at 1d		1	0
Wid Shephard 12 at 5d.		5	0
Edw Polth 12 at 2d.		2	0
John Cockerham 12 at 1½d.		1	6

Daniel Powell 9 at 1d.		9
Capt. Heron 9 at 4d.	4	0
Meritts Tenements 12 at 1d.	1	0
	16	3

1732. To the Newport singers	1	1	0
To the Master teaching three Boys		15	0
For moving goods from the Alms House to Woodside and back again ..		7	0
Exps: at a Meeting to place out Parish Children		6	0
1734. Received by the Old Bible	1	5	0
Gave by order to the Prince of the Moranites		10	6
(A sect of the Syrian Christians).			
Mr. Blake of Sarum for mending the Chalice	1	16	0
To the Church Bible	5	0	0
Repairing the two Palls	3	3	10
1736. 1d. rate rose from £5 6s. 9d. to £16 18s. 8d.			
1736. A cloth for the Communion Table	3	8	3
For a silver salver	4	0	10
For beer when the Engin was mended the first time		2	0
1739. For a New surplice	3	10	6
Making same		10	0
Window curtains and making		14	3
To John Suffield for making two doors measuring 9 yards at 1s. 6d. per yard ..		13	6
To Mr. Beeston towards putting the town pump in order in case of fire ..		9	7
1740. For ringing on Admiral Vernons destroying the forts and castles at Cathagena		10	0
Mr. Payne for cutting Trees in Churchyard		3	0
Paid at several times playing the engine and moving him to and fro from the Guard House		5	0
Paid for a tarpaulin and fixing him on the Scuddle upon the Tower		2	6
1746. Cutting Trees in the Churchyard		9	6
To Mr. Fishlake for an Act of Parliament against swearing			9
1747. Charles Lyne for Crying down Cockskailing and stealing Hedgewood ..		1	0
Gave to poor Sailors more		2	0
1748. For soldiers and sailors coming out of prison at several times		13	7½

Soldiers and Sailors when disbanded were given passes by the local justices, to beg their way home from parish to parish.

For stone for healing the Church	7	0
Paid for Holland and thread to mend the surplice	1	0
For playing the Engine several times and keeping same full	7	1½

1754. Thomas Wimbolt – Minister.

1755. Paid to two sick sailors at *The Horseshoes*	3	0
Paid to a ringing day upon his Majesty's arrival from his Germanic Dominion	6	8

1759. Expenses at *The New Inn* Easter Tuesday	3	3
For a Book for the Clarke		6
A letter from Winchester		3
Relieved two French Prisoners with a pass	2	0
Mending the window shutters of the Church	1	0

1760. Grubbing the Woods in the Churchyard	16	6
Twenty four French prisoners relieved	14	0
Repairing the Great Bell	5	6
A Lock for the Church Door	1	3

1763. To Cutting wood and making new walk in the Churchyard	9	3
Paid Giles Clark of ½ Bushel of wheat	2	0
Paid the Cryer for forbidding shaving on the Sabbath		6
To the hire of a boat to Portsmouth with an appeal concerning John Bampton's family	5	0
A Lock for the Blindhouse Door	2	6
A Line for the Top of the Font in the Church		6
Paid William Sheppard for making a Rate and stating the accounts as usual	12	0

1764. To cash paid in the course of the year for care of the Engine		6	10½
Expenses taking out the engine to lodge a parcell of strollers in the night and guard		2	0
To objects of compassion passing the town		7	6
To Wm Shepards Family in their several Distresses		4	0
For mending the Church hatch		1	8

1765. To Horsehire and Turnpikes	6	2
Paid William Pitt for Cleaning the Church to receive the Bishop	8	0

1766. Exp: at 1st Visitation	1	3	0
Court Fees		5	0
Horsehire and Turnpike		7	0
Mr. Wimbolt (Vicar)		10	6
Penticost fees		1	7
A book of the New Version of Psalms for the Clerk of the Church		3	6
William Pitt for collecting the Church rates		5	0

	£	s	d
1767. To County Bridge Money	4	7	9
1769. Paid Mr. Bedford for serving the Church Six months	31	11	6
Collected	31	5	9
Defficient		5	9
To Wm Wran going to Gosport for Mr. Bedford..		8	6
1770. To expenses selling the seats	1	4	0

(The first mention of the sale of seats.)

	£	s	d
1. The third seat in middle isle from the Pulpit westwards (for life)	16	5	0
2. The 4th seat adjoining above	17	6	0

Note name in book *Abigail Sheppard*.

	£	s	d
1772. To Mr. Groves Man when married by order of ye Parish	3	3	0
To a marriage Register for the Minister		8	6
By Miss Laura Burrard's Burial in Church		6	8
By Three fines for non accepting of Parish Children	30	0	0
1773. To a soldiers wife			6
Paid the Men when about with the Engine		6	3
Advanced more than the subscription came to for ye Engine	2	4	6
Postage of Letters concerning the Engine		1	8
Wharfage of the Engine		1	0
Cleansing the Bucketts and Oil after they were used at Woodman's		1	0
1774. To Thomas Bran three days work		3	0
To the men drawing the River for Gillingham		10	0
Carriage of Tiles, Turnpike and Dam		4	0
Wm Woodman for spun yarn		2	5½
22 yrds of green chiney at 1s. 3d.	1	8	5½

(A plain weave fabric made with fine yarn).

	£	s	d
25½ yds. of Lace		2	10
Mrs. Brice for making the Curtains and Rings		4	9
100¼ of tiles at 2s. 0d.		2	6
To a Broom			1½
To a Dust pan			8
Mr. Couchin for a Bason and Carriage		2	2
Long Lawn for the surplice		6	0

(A very fine linen cloth, now known as Linen Lawn).

	£	s	d
Polly Nash for mending the surplice		2	0
5 yards of Ferrott			10

(Narrow tapes made from floss silk in Italy and France).

	£	s	d
Making three bags for the Communion plate		1	0

Surveying the Bells	2	0
Advertising the Church Plate in the Salisbury Journal	4	0

1774. The Salisbury Journal was then the only county paper. London papers on account of heavy postage were almost unknown and probably not one was taken in the town.

1776. For a chaise to the Visitation		13	0
(First mention of chaise).			
Expenses to Southampton and Winchester going for a Minister	3	12	6
To the Rev. Mr. Jackson at three several times	3	3	0
Horsehire to Milton..		2	7
Horsehire to Milford			7
To the Rev. Richards	1	1	0

1777. Thomas Bargus - Minister.

1777. Mr. Richards for his sermon New Year's Day	1	1	0
To tacking the surplices		1	0
To Cake at the Confirmation		7	0
1778. Paid Bower forbidding the bonfire Crownation Day			6
1d. rate produced	18	7	7½

1779. To crying the Engine to be supplied with water			6
To cutting the weeds in the Churchyard		3	0
To the ringers on the news of the victory over the French and Spanish Fleets ..		10	0

This was the victory of Admiral Hardy and was a time of great rejoicing, as a landing had hourly been expected.

To James Winsey for mending the Engine	18	6
To Spent at Mrs. Webbs at trying the Engine	3	6

1780. To Malt and Hops for the singers	10	5
Received of Mr. Mcilwain for breaking the ground in the Church for a young		
Lady	13	4
Spent at *The Angel* Easter Tuesday	2	6

1780. To a Hook to cut the Trees in the Churchyard	1	3
To moving the Engine and Buckets to the Church		8
Expenses into the Island with Mr. Hicks on Wimbleton's affairs	6	0
To a coach to the Visitation	15	0

1781. To a New form of Prayer for the Fast			6
For the Church Bible and carriage	3	12	8
To a Ribbon for the Ministers Book			4
To four men going about with the Engine		6	0
To the Bellman		1	6

	£	s	d
To an Almanac			7
To Charcoal for the Church			3
1782. To a Bassoon for the singers	1	11	6
3d. rate produced	55	18	0
Non-collections	9	8	3
Cash received	46	9	9
1783. Candlesticks for the Pulpit		10	6
Oct. 1st. To a license for Mr. Bargus on account of the stamps		6	0

This was the stamp duty of 3d. imposed by act of Parliament on all entries on the Parish Registers, baptisms, marriages and deaths, except in cases of extreme poverty.

	£	s	d
1784. Spent at a Meeting of the singers		5	10
Ellis Jones – Minister.			
Spent collecting the rates		2	0
To a Bass Viol	1	12	6
Repairing musical Instruments in the Church			10
1785. Spent in regulating the singers		7	3
Paid to the Cryer for the Church gates being broke			6
Saml Shepard carr of Bells to the Quay		6	0
Paid Capt. Footner of Bells to London	1	7	6
Paid Jos Green for Beer when taking down the Bells		5	10
Paid Mr. Wells Bellfounder	116	1	4
Paid Mr. Wells Bellfounder	8	7	6

	£	s	d
1786.Paid for cleaning the Churchyard and clootting the second floor in the Belfry		7	6
Saml Shepard two loads of Clotty from Waterford		3	0
Spent at signing a Church rate		5	0
Spent electing a Clerk and Sexton		14	6
1789. Repairing a seat in the Singers Gallery		1	6
Mr. West for new hanging the Great Bell		10	6
1790. Carriage to Lyndhurst in Kingaties Van		4	0
Expenses at Lyndhurst		5	0
1791. Twelve books for the singers		6	0
Beer for Ringers binding the New ropes		2	0
Malt and hops for the singers	1	0	6
Spent with workmen when surveying the Church		2	1
1792. A boy delivering summonds to the Committee			6

Paid for a stove for the Vestry	9	0
A Tin Fender	2	9
A Blower for ye Vestry	1	9
A sifter and a poker	2	9
Geo Bran digging four loads of sand	1	4
4 Bushels of coal	3	8

1793. Two chairs for the Vestry	10	6
For a sail cloth to cover the Engine	7	0
A bottle of pepper mint and biskets at selling the seats	2	0

Every kind of parish business called for a bottle or two of something over the pipes of the company.

Spent at *The Bugle* when the rate was confirmed		10	6
Expended on account of signing the Petition for a Faculty		2	6
A Chaise to Winton to confirm the Rate in Court		16	0
Hay and Corn		2	4
Turnpike		1	6
Horseler			8
Expended at Winchester and on the road	1	2	6

1792. A small gallery formerly existed on the North side of the Church extending *in front of two large Pillars*. In this year it was resolved to enlarge this North Gallery, taking away the *large Pillar opposite the pulpit* together with the party wall adjoining same, apparently extending to the *Singing Gallery* and *removing the arch in this gallery*. At the same time a new Vestry room was built in the Churchyard at the East end adjoining the North Chancel window, the Vestry had previously been within the walls of the Church.

The cost of these alterations amounted to about £700 towards which £126 was raised by subscriptions and £600 by sale of seats, the highest sum paid being £40 by Mr. John Fielder for seat No. 14.

1794. Mr. Saml Elgar for a new gate etc.		15	0
One pair Brass Arms and carr for the Pulpitt	2	15	6

June 12th. To the Ringers on the Glorious Victory over the fleet of the French

Convention by Lord How on the 1st June	6	8

1795. Paid for a letter respecting the use of Rice for Flour and starch ..	10

This was an endeavour to get people to economise in bread making owing to the high price of cereals. It is said that from this time it became a habit to bring the loaf onto the table, for the same reason.

1796. Books and stands for the singers	13	0
Mrs. Munt for writing Musick for ditto	12	0
Five copies of Hair Powder list	5	6

		£	s	d
Paid for fixing same at Church and Market Place			1	6
Spent adjusting, parish papers etc.			2	2
A 1d. rate produced approximately in this year		20	0	0
To a place in the stage for one Churchwarden to Southampton			5	6
To a poor woman, to convey her to Portsmouth			2	6
Spent at putting out apprentices			4	0
1797. Mr. Tarver to Winton for Coroner			10	6
Jury for Roger's son drowned			8	0
Cart and Horse to Yeovil to remove Harry Thorne		1	15	0
Expenses to and from Yeovil		2	9	6
Cake 5s. 3d. Wine 9s. 0d. at Confirmation			14	3
1798. Chaise to Southampton		1	4	0
Turnpike and driver			4	0
Court fees			5	0
Procuation			1	11½
1799. Paid two men for Nelson's Victory illuminating the Tower			3	0
For a sett of strings for the Violincello			4	7
To Charles Lane repairing the Bass Viol			12	0
Cash received (rates) for Barracks on Quay			7	0
Ringers on surrender of Dutch Fleet			6	8
1800. Spent at confirming the Rate			8	0
Washing the Pews after the whitewashing			18	0
Balance due to Churchwardens on account of Chandelier			4	0
Expenses going on board a ship to examine respecting a child's death			4	0
Postage of a letter from Winton				6
To Parkin's Girl ill			1	5
and a cart to carry her home			2	0
Two poor Objects in distress			2	0
1801. Mr. Bestland for writing music				8
Repairing the Bass Viol and new hair for bow			3	0
Ringers at the victory of Copenhagen			5	0
Expenses cleaning the Bone hole			3	0
Received of Mr. John Jones for a Pew leased to him and his assigns for ninety nine years		17	0	0
1802. Ringers at proclamation of Peace			10	6
Paid for hoisting Colours on Town hill			2	6
Gloves for Elford cutting nettles			1	0
Four matts for the Church Doors			13	6

Mr. Wells for recasting two and repairing the handbells	2	0	8
1803. Paid Rev. Mr. Jones for feed of Churchyard	1	1	0
1807. 4 Bushels of Coal		6	0
1816. A Crimson velvet cushion for the pulpit	6	6	0
A covering for ditto		3	0

1811. *South Gallery built.*

Mr. Footner for seven lime tree butts	2	12	6
Mr. Blake for Elm timber and butts	6	9	6
£1300 received for New Pews and rate of 6s 6d. = £993	2293	0	0
1815. Received of Mr. James Mew for a seat in Church	36	0	0
Spent at Mr. Mews on receiving his purchase money for a seat		6	0
1816. An Iron Chest	4	4	0
By the Registration Act of 1812			
Burial in Church (last)		13	4
Screw for the viol		1	0
1817. Mr. Joseph Gatrell pounding donkeys		1	0

1820–21. Churchyard altered.

1821. The singers attending at Consecration of New Burial Ground	1	10	0
Ringers at ditto	1	0	0
Expenses for Bishop in Vestry		1	6
Paid G. P. Klitz on Double Bass	13	13	6
1826. Watching the Churchyard		15	0
For seeds		3	6
1828. Expenses at perambulating the Boundaries of the Parish	6	11	2
1834. James Tarver for attending the fire in the Organ		6	3

Old Churchyard

    Till 1821 from centre of present High Street to the centre path from New Lane to Cricket Field.

In 1821 ¾ of acre was added to the North.

Population 1811 = 2641
           1820 = 3164

The New Churchyard of 1859
from Churchwarden's Vestry Book No. 5

Population 4164.

Deaths in District average 91
Churchyard Burials 68

Area of New Ground one acre
450 feet from High Street
194 feet from isolated House to East
291 feet from Ancient Tenement opening direct into the Churchyard (Church Hatch).

Total subscriptions £530
    Land   £278
    New Wall   £160

1833.

On the retirement of the Rev. Ellis Jones in 1833, a vestry resolution was passed to the effect that the Incumbent next chosen should pledge himself to perform Three services on Sunday viz: Prayers and Sermon in the morning (sacrament Sunday excepted), Prayers in the afternoon and prayers and sermon in the evening. So long as the subscription shall amount to £120 p.a. but falling short of this sum the Minister shall be at liberty to relinquish one service, continuing to give two sermons each Sunday (except on the Sacrament Sunday).

1852.

At the time of the appointment of the Rev. B. Maturin the clerk to the Vestry wrote to one of the applicants:–

As regards the Income attached to or derived from the Curacy, I am desired to inform you it is precarious and fluctuating being mainly dependent in voluntary subscriptions from the Inhabitants.

List of Books to 1860
Four Books Letter A Orders to Vestry etc.
1, 2 and 3 Expenditure of Parish 1669 – 1798.
Highway accounts separate from 1767 and continued in five books:–
1767 – 1796   1796 – 1805   1805 – 1814   1814 – 1827   1827 – 1836
Highway Rate Books from 1821 on Highway accounts and duties by paid officers from 1836 – 1847 and from 1847 by two officers chosen.

Overseers accounts separate 1774 – 1827 in seven books
Vestry Books kept distinctly from 1791 in 5 books.
Church Rates kept separate from 1806 – 1854 in three books
Churchwardens separate accounts are from No. 4
    1798 - 1845   1845 - 1856
Poor rates separate from 1776 in eleven books to 1835

The Old Vestry
 Vestry Meeting January 18th 1793.

Resolution 6.
 That at the time the Churchwardens decide who should have each seat – the Vestry Room should be left to themselves and Vestry Clerk.
 Note on Plan of Pews dated 1863 – Nos. 99, 100 and 101 are probably the seats referred to as the repewing of this part of the Church was not carried out till after 1873 – the old high pews still remaining till that date.

Interior of St Thomas' Church. This arrangement of high pews and the three decker pulpit dates this painting to the first part of the 19th century.

Quay Hill *c*.1900. It is interesting to compare this photograph with the earlier one on page 16. This was very much a residential area at this time – witness the large number of young children.

Lymington's first purpose built Post Office in 1865. Head Postmaster Mr Watterson, without a hat, poses with his postmen in front of No. 84, High Street.

CHAPTER TEN

I Remember

I was born in the reign of Queen Victoria, so now I am an old man (but won't admit it). My memory is good as I well remember being put in a cot at two years old and other childish things that we won't bother about.

I first went to school when I was six years old to Mrs. Badcock's school for girls—her husband Henry was the town chemist whose shop was at what is now Maxwell-Hamilton's Sports Shop. Here I was taught to read and write and knit small articles, my greatest achievement being a pair of woollen slippers for my mother. I have never forgotten the art.

When eight years old I was sent to Mr. Murdoch's academy for boys at Stanwell House. Mr. Murdoch was a fierce venerable old gentleman with long white whiskers who had taught my father when he was a boy. Here I lived a life of terror as he kept a huge bundle of canes in the corner and was extremely free with them. Some were mere holly sticks trimmed down but with the knots still protruding were extremely painful when used. I once saw a big boy thrashed with extreme force and much to my admiration he took it without wincing.

Despite all this we all mourned when the old man died. He was honoured and respected by everyone.

Lymington was an entirely different place in those days (1900). There were of course no motor cars. I well remember the first one seen in Lymington (about 1902). It stopped outside *The Angel* and soon had an enormous crowd around it. A few years after, when a few more were on the roads, we boys collected car numbers but progress was slow and we soon gave it up. There was no tar on the roads and the hedges in the country were white with dust all the summer, no green to be seen at all. How different it all is today.

The general conveyance for the gentry were carriages—open landaus, the owners lying back on their padded seats. A carriage and pair was of course the height of opulence, single horse broughams being somewhat looked down upon in consequence. The carriage and pair carried a coachman and footman both wearing cockades in their hats and the latter sitting bolt upright beside the driver with his arms crossed and elbows at right angles. When stopping the footman would swing himself off and dash to the horses' heads holding a bit in each hand. This of course meant that the parcels had to be carried from the shop by the assistant, who had to deposit them on the front seat, and after bowing would retreat backwards towards the shop. You never turned your back to the customer.

Shopping did not generally start before 11 a.m. as no one who professed to be a lady would show herself in the town before that time.

Shopping too was entirely different from today. I well remember a lady and gentleman visiting us and purchasing say 1d. bottle of ink. When the gentleman put his hand to his pocket to pay, his wife remarked "don't pay, let them put it down"—accounts were always sent out quarterly (not monthly as now) so the wretched shopkeeper was always short of money. I have seen a bill about ten inches long where the total amount came to about 16/–.

The town doctors were Dr. Hill and Dr. Chinery, the first being at Grosvenor House and Dr. Chinery in one of the large houses at Highfield. A doctor's life today must be full of frustrations but nothing compared to the life then. I have known Dr. Hill called out to a confinement at Beaulieu at night and his groom harnessed up the horse in the high dogcart he used. When he got there he was not wanted being too early; no sooner had he got home when old John Pardy arrived on foot having walked from Sway—"Oh sir, could you come and see the wife, she's terrible bad". "I'm damned if I will," said the doctor—The old man turned away to walk home again but of course the doctor went, having harnessed up the horse once more and he picked up old Pardy on the way.

People did not move about so much as they do today. I can truthfully say we knew nearly everyone, even the maids who worked in the houses, we knew the postmen by name, the porters at the station, the coal man, the dustman and a hundred and one others. Today one knows a very limited circle of people. Every policeman too was known to us. How many do you know today?

The captains of the steamboats were Capt. Seymour and Capt. Doe. The first-named had the newer boat the *Lymington* and Captain Doe the old *Mayflower*. The bridge was entirely open to all weathers. The steward on the *Lymington* was Mr. Stratton who lived half way down Station Street on the right and his wife used to provide the teas on board—delicious new bread and jam and prawns, as much as you could eat for 6d. How I loved those teas which commenced as soon as we had left Totland Bay to come home. I think the total fare was 9d. or 1/– each.

Some townspeople had season tickets and used to go over by the 7 o'clock boat and back to breakfast.

The best story I know of Capt. Doe, who looked about 70 with a shaggy beard, is that he is said to have suffered heavily from gout and one winter's day having consumed a quantity of drink to drown the pain set off from Yarmouth on a very dark night. The fog came down when near Lymington river and after a lot of searching he announced to the passengers at large "can anyone see Jack?" Within a few minutes he was well and truly on the mud—on a falling tide and was there all night, his passengers being taken off in the morning.

The quay was not in those days a very salubrious place. There were six or seven public houses within a few yards which catered for the locals and the coal and wood ships that came down from the north. I always liked to see the coal unloaded; a dozen or more men each carried a basket skip and would run down one plank and up the other—everything was done on the run—exhausting work!

There being no national health or allowances if you were out of work, men would take anything to earn a living. I have known three or four men row from Lymington to meet the coal boat from Newcastle at Cowes to get signed on to lift the cargo—first come first served.

The Ship inn was then a mean little pub about where the hotel entrance is now. The rest was a warehouse.

To go by ferry boat, huge cumbersome boats, was a ½d to the jetty just behind the railway bridge or 1d to Old Ferry House, but few people had the pluck to ask for this longer journey as it was hard work against the tide.

How different is the river today. I well remember that the first mooring after the pier was opposite the Coastguard Station (now the Royal Lymington Y.C.) and that was always occupied by the Coastguard cutter. From there to the end of the river there were not more than a dozen yachts. The number in the river today must be between 1000–1500. Is it true that 90% never leave their moorings?

At the time of the Boer War I well remember the Yeomanry. I suppose the local force amounted to a troop, the horses being usually used to draw the tradesmen's vans. I don't think many could ride properly–most were stout and portly in build and it was even said they had to be hoisted into the saddle. In any case they made a splendid martial sight riding in their resplendent uniforms, which reminds me that during the Boer War a man called Kellaway, an assistant at Purchases (now Oakeshotts[1]) volunteered for the front. He was solemnly marched down to the station headed by the Town Band with hundreds of people to see him off–few men could have gone to serve their country with such a magnificent send-off.

Then there was the annual circus. It started with a parade through the town at about 12.30; first came the circus band seated in a waggon drawn by four horses with the drum fastened to the back, then the star attraction—a huge waggon drawn by six or eight horses with an erection on it built in pyramid fashion of steps—each draped with girls in spangled tights while at the very top about twenty five feet from the ground was a beautifully dressed girl. To me this was a breath-taking sight but I suppose these beautiful damsels were in reality only the gypsy type cleaned and dressed up.

Then came the animals in cages—lions and tigers, monkeys and elephants and to my joy each one holding the tail of the one in front. There were the clowns and acrobats too, the whole procession being some ½ mile or so long. All this of course was to advertise the evening show in a large marquee in Gas Works field (now built over). How I pity children to-day who have never seen such marvellous sights.

In winter after a hard frost, we all used to cycle over to Hatchet Pond and skate until we were exhausted and for amusement in the town we had a roller skating club at the Malt Hall

---

1   25, High St. Now a supermarket.

(now the Community Centre). The floor there was concrete and we suffered agonies if we sat down, which was often. Still, we all soon became extremely efficient doing intricate turns to gramophone music. I would here like to stress that the young people found their own amusements—nothing was provided for them.

As far as I remember we had one yearly dance at the Literary Institute, to which everybody went. There were no cinemas.

We do not seem to have the characters in the town today that we once had; the following story may amuse you, it is true because it was told me by one of the gentlemen concerned. A Lymington gentleman did not drink locally, presumably because his good name would suffer if seen visiting hotels. It was the same for a well-known gentleman from Milford, so every day they each set out to walk the four miles, one to drink at *The Red Lion*, Milford and the other at *The Angel*, Lymington. As each set off at 11 a.m. to be in time for opening at 12 they would daily pass each other half way at Everton. In course of time they knew each other very well and would quip "Good morning Mr. — are you going down for your glass of milk?"

I also know two prominent tradesmen who one day, after a heavy snowstorm, tobogganed down the town hill on a large tea tray. These things don't seem to happen today and consequently life is the poorer.

About sixty years ago when the old Borough Council was in existence, we had two councillors one was a very large man, a butcher and the other a much smaller man, a grocer. They were great friends until one day they disagreed on some council matter and the grocer was so upset that having consumed a lot of liquor he retired to bed, but the quarrel praying on his mind he got up at midnight and taking a large bacon knife from the counter went to his friend's house intending to settle the point finally.

Luckily the butcher had two large sons who threw him out and so saved a tragedy. We had a lot of fun and excitement in those days.

Churchgoing was a must in my boy-hood days. Our own seat was just outside the vestry door and the Perrys sat opposite in the corner, then came the Badcock family and then the John Kings—these seats then all facing the pulpit—the church was full every Sunday. The sermons usually preached by old Canon Maturin were long and the prayers including the Litany seemed to me as a boy, endless. On a hot summer day I used to watch through the south door, old Mr. Osey loading up his milk cans from Aldridges Dairy (now Ford's). The choir sat in the gallery next to the organ so there was little singing in the body of the church beyond a dull murmur—anyone raising their voices in song were looked at in some astonishment. Mr. Murdoch and his boarders sat in the gallery in the front seat overlooking the pulpit. On Sunday evenings the Salvation Army met in a circle outside the Steven Worner's Furniture shop and then marched with flag flying to their barracks in Emsworth Road (now a sale room) with a small following bringing up the rear.

People today do not walk as they once used to. When I was a boy I knew every road and footpath within four miles of the town. Some walks today are quite impossible. There was even a beautiful way undershore past the Gas works right through to Ampress by the river side but this is now overgrown with trees and quite impossible to get through. When our first

Artesian well was being sunk, about 1904? I used to walk almost daily with my father who was then on the Corporation to watch progress and well remember when the first water was struck at about 150 feet. It came gushing out of the grownd into large settling tanks without any pumping and in one of the bores the engineers brought up three sharks teeth. My father had them made into brooches for my sisters. It is a strange thought that say a million years ago we had sharks in Lymington.

All the roads were then untarred, they were extremely muddy and one's shoes or boots were caked in mud up to the ankles; it was very necessary then to have scrapers outside ones house to remove as much mud as possible. If you walk down Captains Row (then called South Street) and Nelson Place you can still count up to a dozen scrapers outside the houses, some just a plain piece of iron fixed to the railings and some more elaborate (and costly). These little things can tell you much of what our forebears used to have to put up with.

Our income as a family was then small by today's standards but we managed to live quite comfortably. We had a cook, Ester Pardy, a nursemaid, Fanny Pardy and a house boy, Johnny Pardy, they came from a large family at Sway and as soon as one left to get married another of the family would take her place. I had four sisters and so we were a large family and this staff had plenty to do. Few people today can afford to keep even one maid sleeping in. As far as I remember, wages were £10 a year.

The toll bridge across the river in 1906. The first toll bridge was built in 1735 by Captain Cross. The latter had inherited the site from a relative favoured by Charles II with land grants which included all the mudlands between Calshot and Hurst Castle.

Lymington's first hospital opened on April 9, 1913. All the funds required for its foundation, and several subsequent extensions were raised by public subscription.

The town mill and the tidal mill pond which was next to the river approximately where the railway station is today.

This fine terrace of thatched houses in Belmore Lane burnt down in 1908 resulting in the destruction pictured below. The Millwrights Arms pub can be seen on the right of the lower photograph.

The old toll house behind what was The Crown Inn and is now The Tollhouse Inn, in deference to its former historic role. The Sway road snakes away in the background.

The Anchor and Hope Inn in the High Street. Known originally as The Crown, it was destroyed by fire in 1905. The shop premises to the left in this photograph are at 95, High Street.

CHAPTER ELEVEN

The Inns of Lymington

I compiled this list some years ago, so many of the licences having been revoked, it was very necessary to list them before all traces had been lost.

In each case I have only recorded the first landlords known to me as the list of the others running into hundreds of names would occupy too much space and be of little interest to others.

ALARM INN
Position—On the right hand corner of Quay Hill at its junction with Quay Street.
Named after *The Alarm* yacht built by Thomas Inman for Mr. Weld of Pylewell in 1830.
Closed January 27th, 1923.
The landlady in 1869 was Mary Ann Cowndley.

THE ALBION INN
Position–Built well back from the street on the site of the present Masonic Hall.
The Thrings were an eccentric family–William (senr) Landlord 1851 practised inoculation against smallpox, not very successfully. The daughters were straw bonnet makers. William Thring was also a Vestry Clerk.
When the house was demolished, the materials were used to build the Theatre at pierside (Capt. Jobbling). The Misses Thring retired to a house at the end of Madeira Walk.
Closed 1880.
The landlord in 1836 was James Farmer.

ANGEL HOTEL
Originally called *The George* and as it was so called before the accession of George I to the throne, it was probably named after the patron saint St. George.

1673. A tenement containing a hall and a shop with a chamber over, commonly called *The Angel*, was leased by Bartholomew Bulkeley (lord of the manor) to Edward Smith for a term of 2000 years.

The Angel is believed to have taken its name from this house which was the second tenement on the left-hand side of Navarino Court.

1675. Earliest mention as *The George* in the Borough books when a licence of 4d. was paid for a sign, equivalent today to about 10/–.

1756. Called *The Angel* in a letter from the Southampton Corporation to Thomas Shepard, Mayor of Lymington asking him to dine there with the Mayor of So'ton, George West.

1762. Called *The Angel* inn—The Court Leet was held here on October 12th in that year.

1775. J.H. (John Hannaford). This mark appears on the wall of the Garage (then a coach house) on the right hand side.

1780. From the Vestry accounts. "Spent at *The Angel*, Easter Tuesday 2/6". This was the passing over of the Account Books to the new Churchwardens and was always held at an Inn on Easter Tuesday of each year, the sums expended in ale and tobacco on these occasions varies considerably.

1782. Rowlandson stayed here on his famous tour and sketched *The Angel* frontage, the yard, the kitchen, the "pretty Landlady", a fruit shop and the Quay.

In the old coaching days the "Royal Mail Coach" left here at 4.45 every evening.

The Landlord in 1777 was John Hannaford.

ANCHOR AND HOPE

Formerly known as *The Crown*.

From an old deed:—"All that messuage or tenement, stable near and garden thereunto belonging and adjoining situate lying and being on the north side of the High Street of Lymington formerly called or known by the name of *The Crown* but now *The Anchor and Hope* formerly in the tenure of Jane Cooper and now of Edward Webster."

1905. The old building was burnt down in this year.

1951. The neck of a large jar with the name "Wm Ackland" on the side (see list of landlords) is now in my possession, this was found on the site of the Council Houses, being built on the South side of Union Hill, (now East Hill) during excavations.

In Coaching days "The Telegraph" coach left from here every day at 5 a.m. and the "Commercial" Coach from *The Star* Hotel, Southampton 8 a.m. called here at 10.30 and proceeded via Mudeford, Christchurch, Poole, Wareham and Dorchester reaching Weymouth at 7 p.m.

1802. A Vestry Meeting held on February 25 was adjourned to the House of Mrs. Rachael Robinson at the sign of *The Anchor and Hope*.

1805. Vestry meeting again adjourned here—the landlord Jarvis Harbin was one of the Overseers of the poor for the year.

1815. Received of Mr. James Mew for a seat in the Church £36. Spent at Mr. Mews on receiving his purchase money for a seat 6/–.

The landlady when known as *The Crown* was Jane Cooper.

BOROUGH ARMS

Established in 1855 as a Posting House.

1858. Known as *The Clipper Arms*.

The landlord in 1859 was James Joliffe.

BRITTANIA

Position—Station Street.

Built about 1870 on a piece of waste land which was used for Entertainments.

The landlord in 1872 was William Reeks.

THE BUGLE

The name is a corruption of Bubale a species of wild bull and for long the sign was that of a Bulls Head to the bewilderment of the towns folk.

1675. Mentioned in the Borough Books as paying 4d for the sign in that year.

1707. May 20. A Parish Meeting held at Mr. Wrights at *The Bugle* (from the Vestry Accounts)

1793. July 7th. "To spend at *The Bugle* when the rate was confirmed 10/6 (from the Vestry) Accounts).

1814. Beer provided for the Peace Celebrations of July 7th of that year. (The Peace of Amiens)

The landlady in 1707 was Mrs. Wright.

CHEQUERS

Position—Woodside.

The sign of *The Chequers* probably the oldest in the world as a chequer sign was found during the excavation of the ruins of Pompeii. In early days it denotes any house where money transactions were made but our local sign is probably derived from the fact that the Salt Exchequer Offices had their headquarters at Lower Woodside Green.

One of the few local Inns known to have had a skittle alley.

The landlord in 1791 was James Viney.

CROWN INN

Position—Buckland.

A very old roadside Inn, with the old Toll House standing a few yards away to the North.

The name may come from the royal crown of England or from being placed on the crown of the hill. In the old coaching days it is probable that the heavy coaches and waggons stopped here to rest their horses after the long pull up hill.

1764. August 16th. The Freemason's Lodge was constituted here.

During the time of Stephen Harris (1877) monkeys were kept here.

The landlord in 1836 was John Etheridge.

CROWN AND ANCHOR

Position Captains Row.

Rebuilt 1889 or 1899 (To date of rebuilding was a beerhouse).

Captain Stains was skipper of the "Silver Star" built here'.

Originally occupied No. 1 Captain Row and later included No. 2. When it was rebuilt it occupied Nos. 1, 2, 3 and 4.

The landlord in 1861 was Henry Rice.

THE DOLPHIN

Formerly known as *The Blue Anchor* then *The Railway Inn*.

Position—On the right hand side of Quay Street opposite *The Yacht Inn*—now in the occupation of Mr. Renouf. One of the few local Inns known to have a skittle alley.

1814. Beer provided for Peace Celebrations of July 7th in that year "The Peace of Amiens".

Licence expired July 11th 1911 when premises closed as a Licenced House.

A landlady of *The Blue Anchor* was Francis Gray (widow).

Jonah Rickman became the landlord in 1858 when it was known as *The Railway Inn* and in 1883 the landlord of *The Dolphin* was Henry William St. John.

DORSET ARMS

Position—St. Thomas Street.

Formerly known as *The Fighting Cocks*.

1836. William A. Green.

Rebuilt September 1882. Named changed to *The Dorset Arms*. The landlord was Thomas Collingwood.

DUKES HEAD.

The Old Coastguard Station at The Salterns—now Dukes Head Cottages No 3.

Probably named after the Duke of Wellington. Re-built in 1824. Probable date of closing

1870. Evidence: George (Monsey) Bran was born in 1859 and he just remembers the house being open when a boy.

The landlady in 1841 was Maria Ninian.

FISHERMANS REST

The Fishermans Rest was granted first Licence in 1870.

Position—Woodside.

This was formerly a cottage. The first licence was granted to James Bran, the father of George (Monsey) Bran in 1870 who was followed by his two sons. John Bran (of 1903) was a nephew of James and John and George Edward were the sons of John.

Smuggling was carried on in James Bran's time and George remembers seeing one of the small three gallon kegs used for this purpose. (1951 George Bran now 92 years).

In 1852 the house was called Grattens Cottage.

James Bran was the landlord in 1870.

GREYHOUND

Position not known with certainty but probably in Gosport Street.

1814. July 7th. Beer provided for the Peace Celebration (The Peace of Amiens).

The landlord was James Smith.

THE HARLEQUIN

Position—the last house on right in Bath Road after the Shipyard and next to the Council Houses.

A ferry once went from here to Blakes Dock on the opposite shore now the site of Lymington Pier.

Reported as being the headquarters of the Press Gang.

The landlord in 1847 was James Cott.

HEARTS OF OAK

Formerly *The Blacksmith's Arms* then *Foresters Arms*.

In 1800 this was the first house in Lymington to meet the traveller's eye after passing the Old Manor House, Buckland. The Stocks and the public well stood at the present entrance to the Sports Ground.

1814. Beer provided for Peace Celebrations of July 7th (Peace of Amiens).

This Inn was first called *The Blacksmiths Arms* and John Marshall was the landlord in 1836. Later it became *The Foresters Arms* and in 1859 John Rogers became the landlord. Finally, in 1878 the name changed to *The Hearts of Oak* with Edward Charles Meadows becoming the landlord.

ISLE OF WIGHT HOY
   Position—In Gosport Street on site of Tillers Nurseries, now Trafalgar Houses. Built approx 1600–1640. Removed mid 19th Century.
   A "Hoy" was a large one-decked boat, commonly rigged as a sloop.
   Probably the nautical cry "Ship Ahoy" comes from the boat which is Dutch in origin.
   The landlord in 1836 was William Lawrence.

KING'S ARMS
   Position—St. Thomas Street.
Traditional: A room in the old Inn was reported to have been occupied by Charles I.
   (Traditon is not to be despised—E. Hapgood).
   It is more probable that the Inn dates from the reign of Charles II as the "King's Arms" were set up in the Church in 1676.
1814.   The Inn provided Beer for the Peace Celebrations of July 7th. (The Peace of Amiens).
   John Bright became landlord in 1791.

KING'S HEAD
   Position—top of Quay Hill.
   The landlord in 1836 was Thomas Avery.

THE LITTLE CROWN INN
   Position not known. From Directory of 1784. James King landlord.

LONDESBOROUGH HOTEL
   Called *The Nag's Head* till September 6th 1884.
1600.   George Truman was fined 3d towards the upkeep of the Towne Well in the Hyghe Streete. He was one of many called upon for this rate the punishment for default being "debbell" payment.
1607.   The same George Truman was in trouble again for upon being requested by the "Bay-liffe" to appear before the Mayor he refused to do so, and was as a user of "Victuallinge and Tiplinge" threatend with the loss of his licence.
1674. Spent at *Nag's Head* £2 3s. 7d. on the occasion of the Dutch War.
1675.   The fee of 4d. was paid for the "signe".
1683.   Two watchmen to garde prisoners one night at ye *Nagg's Head* 2/–.
1687.   Paid at two meetings for expenses upon ye Corporation at *Nags Head* 18/–.
1689.   Paid when King William and Queen Mary were proclaimed at ye Market Cross. One hogshead of beere 30/– and at ye *Nags Head* one hoggshead of beere 30/– and for wine, beere and tobacco in at ye *Nags Head* and out at ye Market Cross £4 7s. 0d. and Drummers in all £7 9s. 6d.

1694. Paid at Riggs for Bread and Beere for the prisoners which came from France 4/10 (from Churchwardens Accounts).

1712. Expenses at *The Nags Head* on parish business 2/1 (Churchwardens a/cs).

1727. From the Manor Rolls—Item: We present the chimney in Mrs. Riggs brewhouse very much out of repair and very dangerous as to fire and that the same be sufficiently repaired and secured by the 11th inst. on pain of 20 shillings.

1728. Expenses at ye *Nags Head* with Sir Robert and others in Barth Skeat's affair 2/6. Note:—"Sir Robert" was Sir Robert Smythe Bart of Buckland (Mayor in 1689) who was very constant and active at all parochial and borough meetings. The "others" were the Churchwardens and Overseers who met at *The Nags* Head to debate parish matters over a pipe and a pot of ale.

1729. April 23rd. Expenses at *Nagg's Head* 4/- (Churchwardens a/cs.).

1744. From the Parish Registers of Burials. Thomas Williams (Rigs) known commonly by the name of Farmer Rigs or the Nagshead farmer.

Named changed to *The Londesborough* Hotel in 1884. It is said that Lord Londesborough when staying at Lyndhurst used to drive over to quench his thirst here and the landlord was so honoured that he tore down the old sign.

In Coaching days "The Independent" left from here for Southampton at 5 a.m. every morning arriving there at 7.30 a.m.

The landlord in 1600 was George Truman.

MAYFLOWER
The landlord in 1868 was Charles Baker.

Another landlord, in 1883, was Captain James Cutler who was formerly skipper of the yacht "Rita". These premises closed on July 21st 1927.

The Mayflower Hotel was opened in 1927 when the landlord was Ernest Reginald Wheeler.

MILLWRIGHTS ARMS
Site: In Belmore Road, next door but one to the Mason's Yard.

In 1851 William Bran was a brewer.

Closed, last licence issued February 7th 1915. John Hosey was the landlord in 1836.

NEW INN OR THE YEOMAN
Position not known. Almost certainly Mews Brewery.

1730. From the Vestry Accounts. To Jacob Marks expenses at ye Parish Meeting etc. £2 13s. 8d.

1759. Expenses at *The New Inn* Easter Tuesday. 3/3.

1814. July 7th. Beer provided for the Peace Celebration (Peace of Amiens).

1806. April 8th. A Vestry Meeting held this day, adjourned to *The New Inn*.

The landlord in 1757 was Jacob Marks.

OLD ENGLISH GENTLEMAN[1]

Queen Street. At one time brewed its own beer. James Tarwin became the landlord in 1852.

RAILWAY INN

Dating from the opening of the Railway, July 12th 1858.

Site. The house on the right at Bridge Gates with the Old Station behind it. Licence transferred to *The Railway Hotel* in Station Street, shortly after the new station was built.

RAILWAY HOTEL[2]

In 1863 the landlord of *The Railway Hotel* was William Curtis.

RED LION

A very fine Old Inn, as originally built.

On an old bottle window at the rear of the premises is engraved in very fair lettering "1853 E.F. Gosling" the landlord of that year.

Christopher Fry was the landlord in 1784.

SHIP

In 1805 The Stoney Cellar belonged to *The Ship* inn and was assessed for rating at £4.

The old *Ship* had a six inch board bedded in clay just inside the door to keep out the high tides.

Rebuilt 1936.

The landlord in 1784 was William Bay.

SIX BELLS

Site: St. Thomas Street next to the Church, now the Dairy.

Once the Headquarters of the Bellringers. The Church Tower was built in 1670 and probably the house dates from this time.

1814.   July 7th Beer provided for the Peace Celebrations.

1791.   Paid to John Foot for the Ringers 6/8 (Churchwardens a/cs.).

1795.   To Foot at ye Bells for a Woman in distress 1/6 (Oversees a/cs.).

Closed on December 28th 1911. The landlord in 1790 was a Mr. Rogers.

SLOOP

Site: Exact position not known but was probably over the River.

1814.   Beer provided for Peace Celebrations of 1814.

The landlord in 1791 was Harry Powell.

---

1   Now *The Famous Black Cat*.

2   Now *The Coach House*.

SNOWDROP

Site: At top of Station Street on left side going down at the junction with Gosport Street.

Licence expired July 11, 1911 when premises were closed.
Henry St. John became landlord in 1872.

SOLENT INN

This house when built (about 1700) was a gentleman's residence.
Site: At foot of Quay Hill, facing High Street.

A Bowling Green was at the back of the house and in early days till about 1880 they brewed their own beer.

William Stephen and his wife built "Crown Villa" next to the Methodist Church in Gosport Street. The house was so named because they paid the workman in Crown pieces weekly from their savings.

Closed on February 2nd, 1939. The landlord in 1843 was George Stephens.

THE STAR

Formerly *The Prince of Wales*.
Site. At left side of Cannon Street going up at junction with Gosport Street.

As the sign was the Prince of Wales Feathers, the Inn was known as *The Feathers* and *The Plume of Feathers*.

Closed March 8th 1934. James Granston was the landlord of *The Prince of Wales* in 1847 and Henry Rawlins Bowden became landlord of *The Star* in 1879.

THE SWAN

Site: On Lymington Bridge. Otherwise known as *The Bridge Tavern*.
The Bridge was built in 1731 by Captain Cross.

A very good story of this Inn, is that as the licencing hour was 10 p.m. in Boldre Parish and 11 p.m. in Lymington, its customers would cross a passage, which was reputed to be the dividing line of the parishes and enjoyed themselves for a further hour.

Unfortunately for the story, there was only one licence issued for the house and the boundary of Lymington is actually to the west of the Inn (in Boldre).

When the late Lord Montagu of Beaulieu was driving King Edward VII on his first car ride, they came to the Toll Gate at this Inn. The gate-keeper (the landlord) approached and Lord Montagu called to him "Hurry up and open the gate. Don't you see that His Majesty the King is with me?" "I know them Kings" he replied "Two of your sort slipped by me only this morning. Pay your sixpence first then you'll have to wait there until I've let this donkey cart through". And wait they did—to King Edward's considerable amusement.

Mrs. Cooper (Widow) was the landlady of *The Swan* in 1791 and Thomas James Fripp was landlord of *The Freemans Arms* in 1872.

THREE HORSE SHOES
  Situation on the site of the Lady's Wing, Literary Institute, New Lane. Known at the time
of Closure as *The Blacksmiths Arms* (Mr. Buckler and Mr. Geo. Payne).

1755. From the Churchwardens Accounts: Paid to two sick sailors at *The Horseshoes*, 3/–.
  Closed August 31st 1878 by order of the court for harbouring a Policeman. Mary Best was
landlady in 1841.

TRUE BLUE
  Site not identified.

1814. July 7th. Beer provided for Peace Celebrations (Peace of Amiens).
1819. From the Guardian's Accounts. Paid Russell at *True Blue* for Board of Lodging to
John Gass's wife £1 0s. 0d.
  John Buckett was the landlord in 1806.

WALTHAM ARMS
  Site: At No. 51 High Street.

1904. Fred Beer, the landlord, drove the Londesborough Hotel bus (two horses).
  Closed March 11th 1943. The landlord in 1872 was Charles Olive.

WILLIAM IV
  Afterwards known as *The British Workman.*
  Site: The house after The Dolphin—facing the Quay.

  William IV crowned 1830.

  The landlord of *The William IV* in 1851 was George Rose and when known as *The British
Workman* in 1885 the landlord was Jones Minall.

WATERLOO ARMS
  Formerly *The Bricklayers.*
  Site: On right side of Priestlands Place (formerly known as Soapy Lane or Temple Bar).

1886. From an old deed: All that messuage or tenament being a public house and called or
known by the name of *The Waterloo Arms* formerly called *The Bricklayers Arms* together
with the garden thereunto adjoining and belonging and situate lying and being in Soapey
Lane in the parish of Lymington in the county of Southampton bounded on the east by the
lands of John Rickman on the west by lands called the Roundabout on the north by the
land formerly of Jane Blake widow deceased and on the south by the said lane called Soapey
Lane and now in the occupation of Charles Warner.

1811.   From a handwritten Sale Bill. To be sold by Auction by Mr. Jn Newell on Tuesday the 12th of July, 1811 at *The Bricklayers Arms* about three acres of Meadow Grafs more or less adjoining the lane in Old Town the property of the late Mr. Jn Woodford. Sale at 6 o'clock in the evening.

1814.   July 7th. Beer provided for Peace Celebration.

1815.   Battle of Waterloo.

Notes:—The Warners father and son were both from the Life Guards and were 6 ft. 2 in. tall.

Tom Batts, the landlord, drove the one-horse Mail Van to and from Brockenhurst.
Closed December 28th, 1911. The landlord of *The Waterloo Arms* in 1835 was Henry Prince.

WHITE LION

Site: at 88 High Street, now Klitz's Music Warehouse.

1675.   Mentioned in the Borough Books as paying the sign fee of 4d.

WHEELWRIGHTS ARMS

Site: at the present house standing at north end of Waterloo Road on extreme left hand side.

Evidence: Map of Lymington. Now demolished.

WHEATSHEAF

Built about 1700.

The first meeting of the R.A.O.B. Lodge was held here.

The landlord in 1806 was Thomas Langford.

WAGGON AND HORSES

Formally a thatched Inn, rebuilt in 1908.

Reputed to be the stopping place for waggoners waiting for the ebb tide before crossing the ford, before 1731 when the bridge was built.

The country people left their donkeys and carts here to cross by the ferry for their weekly shopping in the town. Charges, donkey tiedup 1d. stabled 3d.

The old tap room ceiling was covered with coins.

Elgar was the landlord in 1800.

YACHT INN

Site: on corner of Quay and Quay Street across the road from *The Dolphin*.

Closed December 28th 1911. In 1863 the landlord was Thomas Philips.

Kings. Bookseller, Stationer, Engraver and Printer, 105/6 High Street, Lymington. This photograph taken in 1861, shows on the left Edward King (1821 - 1885) author of Old Times Revisited, and Mayor of Lymington in 1871, 1872 and 1878. In the doorway is Charles King and to his left his elder brother Richard. In front of the doorway on the right are three of King's printers – Meadows, Loader and Gatrell.

Edward King (1893 - 1974). Edward, author of this book, was the fourth child but only son of Charles King.

CHAPTER TWELVE

Kings of Lymington

The year 1960 will probably mark the 225th anniversary of our family business as printers, booksellers and stationers, for it was about the year 1735 that John King, the first known member of our family set up his small printing plant in the town of Yeovil, Somerset.

John King was born about the year 1700 and began life as a poor gloving boy in that town.

But before embarking on the story of the business may I take you back a few years from that date to give a background of the conditions prevailing at this period.

In Stuart times printers were deemed to be a somewhat dangerous set of people, for the bombardment of political pamphlets and broadsheets that were in circulation at this period so alarmed the government of the day that in 1663 the first licensing act was passed. This act was so restrictive that the number of printers in the UK was reduced to 20 and these all in London.

It is said that when William of Orange occupied Exeter in 1688 the capital of the west was unable to furnish a single printer or machine to strike off copies of his manifesto.

The contrast between the year of our foundation 1735 and today is of course immense. The population of England was then only 7 million and hardly one Englishman in ten could read or write.

Few families had more than the Bible, one or two bound books and a few pamphlets in their possession. Newspapers were non-existent ('The Times' not being published till 50 years afterwards in 1785) and news was selected by professional gossip writers who visited the coffee houses of London and sent their letters to country subscribers who passed the sheets from hand to hand among their friends.

Travel was tedious; it took 4½ days from London to Manchester.

It was in these times that John King, my great-grandfather's grandfather was born. He must have been a boy of some talent as family history records that by dint of hard work and study he gradually rose to be a schoolmaster, the best in the town of Yeovil and also had the teaching of the charity school of Nowes, which in those days was attached to the west end of St. Johns Church in the centre of the town.

I have had the good fortune to find the charity books with his signature in beautiful script giving his receipt for his salary – 'Paid to John King for 3½ years teaching 8 boys ending 24th October 1751, £23.15s.4½d'.

It is also recorded in our history that he knew seven languages and added to his income by keeping the parish accounts.

He was a great walker and would walk from Yeovil to Wells, 20 miles each way, to hear divine service at the Cathedral and walk home again. He once walked to Weymouth, 28 miles, to attend morning service, taking his breakfast in his pocket and sitting down in a field to eat it, but the service being half over when he arrived, he stayed the night, got up early and after a bathe in the sea, walked back to Yeovil. Fifty-six miles in two days.

Now as I have already stated the conditions prevailing at the time, it need hardly be repeated that printed matter was hard to come by and his teaching was so restricted thereby that he set up a small handpress and printed a few simple things for the use of the school.

The printer at this time was confined not by lack of orders but by production costs and technical difficulties – all paper was made from rags for cheap woodpulp was still far away.

Such is a brief glimpse of conditions when John started his little business. How completely bewildered he would be if he could but see the developments that two centuries would bring since he began work in his Yeovil printing shop.

He married one of the three daughters of a gentleman named Phelps, a family well-known in Yeovil.

In June of this year I went to Yeovil in order not only to confirm what is written in our family journal but to try if possible to discover more details of the past. In the short space of two days I had unbelievable good fortune.

My first call was at a solicitor's office – Batten and Co – and I found to my astonishment that this solicitor was the brother of the late Colonel Batten of Lymington; they have been in business in Yeovil since about 1720. My second surprise was while in their waiting room to find myself looking at a small black frame containing a sale notice of various plots of land in 1790 with the imprint of John King. This was by far the earliest piece of our work that I had so far found and on my return home I wrote to Mr. Batten asking for the loan.

From the solicitor's office I went to the Museum, which is a fine room over their public library next door to the Town Hall. There the curator, Mr. Batty, showed me a large oil painting of the parish church with the school house adjoining and entitled 'The Master takes his pupils to Church' and dated about 1750. If this date is correct I found myself looking at John King the schoolmaster and printer. The picture represents a tall man in a wig and a tricorn hat of the period and wearing an embroidered robe, followed by 12 or 15 of his pupils going towards the church door.

My third surprise was to follow immediately. It is stated in our family book that due to his marriage into the family of Phelps, a place called George Court came into our family. Upon asking where George Court was likely to be the curator asked me to turn in my chair and look out of the window and there below us was the place I had been looking for. This seemed to me proof that what had been written so many years before was true. John who died in 1762 had three sons. The eldest, also named John, born in 1740, succeeded to the business on his father's death and eventually became Portreeve, otherwise Mayor of Yeovil, seven times, from 1789 to 1796. George was the second son and Charles who eventually came to Lymington.

We will come back to Charles later as it is necessary to tell you that the second son George had four sons; George born 1777 who was not a printer in after life, John who was apprenticed to the business, Edward who became a soldier and fought throughout the Peninsular War as a sergeant major in the Coldstream Guards and Richard, my great-grandfather, born 1796.

There is rather an amusing story attached to John no. 3. He once went to see his son who had opened a business at Newbury, and as an advertisement blew a key bugle outside the shop. This I believe was rather frowned upon by the family but he thought at the time that this was an extremely good piece of advertising and when one thinks it over you are bound to admit that however good or bad an instrumentalist he was it provided a very short cut to becoming well-known in the town. I like to think that this is the origin of the saying 'To blow your own trumpet'.

Richard, my great-grandfather, was born in 1796 and was duly apprenticed to the family business, but at the age of 21 on 4th, April 1817, he set off by road to join his uncle Charles who he had heard of as having gone to Lymington.

Charles had in the meantime been a bookseller in Dorchester where he had a Bookshop opposite the Roebuck and it was there that he is said to have advertised for a wife and was more than fortunate in obtaining a very good one, by name Eleanor Stanley.

He had moved to Lymington in 1805. There was no bookbinder or printer and nothing to speak of as a Bookseller in this town at the time, and so he had all the business of the large number of French Royalists who were concentrated here – four thousand in all besides the English regiments and the local townspeople. It has been recorded that he was so busy that he had to send to London for supplies daily, a most unheard of proceeding in those times.

Richard then set out from Yeovil to join his uncle. He had never seen him or corresponded as letters were expensive in those days; ninepence for a single sheet of paper. He had completed his apprenticeship at Yeovil after much hard work and by sitting up at night to practise the art of setting up posters, and even by bribing a workmate with an old watch to give him a few valuable hints.

One job which he particularly disliked was visiting the country fairs to sell books and riding round the district on horseback collecting accounts. As I have already said he set off walking to Lymington at break of day on 4th, April 1817, two years after Waterloo and getting to Shaftesbury by early afternoon pushed on to Wimborne and put up for the night, 35 miles the first day. The next day on to Lymington via Ringwood, 24 miles – 59 miles in two days. On arrival he called at the *Angel* then kept by a Mrs. Butcher and drinking his glass of ale asked for his uncle and was directed down to 126 High Street.

Richard took himself down the street and into the shop. It was partitioned into a little reading room and in it was a person reading a paper. It was Dr. Towsey (who lived where now the old Police Station is) and who afterwards was to become a great friend of the family. A stout woman was behind the counter and upon his enquiry replied 'and what do you want with him' and on being told became more gracious and directed my great-grandfather to the side door up the yard.

Thus uncle and nephew met and after a meal were soon deep in discussion on the merits of bookbinding. Taking down a little copy of Pope's Homer from the shelf the old man who was now 70 said "there Richard, can you bind like that?" and Richard had to admit that through lack of practice he could not, but would do what he could to improve.

He stayed with his uncle and made himself useful. The binding was done by warming the tools over an open fire on a trivet – gas was unknown and lighting was by candle and the water was drawn from the town well.

Printers and bookbinders toiled from 7 in the morning until 8 at night. Work might stop a little earlier on Saturdays but the only holidays they had were Christmas days and Sundays. He worked hard and soon formed a circle of acquaintances who noticed the improvement in the style of binding. One of the St. Barbes' was one of his patrons. In course of time he married "the girl next door" and the old people retiring to a house up the street Richard stepped out on his own account.

His capital was £100 and with this he had to furnish the shop and set up as a printer and binder, meeting competition from three others who had now arrived in the town. One of these said that he would shut Richard up in six months, a very dangerous statement to make. He determined to try to make a living despite this severe opposition, but indeed with all his energy he might well have failed had he not been favoured by a fortunate chance which has much to do with all human effort.

He went to London by coach, 11½ hours, probably taking the Royal Mail which left at 5.30 p.m. and travelled through the night, to see if he could find some stock and plant suitable for his small means. He had never been to London before. He first looked into the publishers Longmans whose name he had heard of and bought a copy of a popular work of the day – *Broad Grins* by George Coleman. It was a thin foolscap 8vo book and cost 6/- and strange to say that this first book he bought never sold. He looked at it ruefully and wondered how he was going to fill his shelves and buy materials with his poor £100. In this mood he walked up Cheapside looking for goods to buy.

He passed a shop just by Bow Church where there were a number of people collected and an auction seemed to be going on. To his great surprise he found that it was an auction of books. He was completely astonished for he saw bundles of good books being sold for mere trifles. He bid, bought a few lots and they appeared to be all right. The auctioneer called him aside, found out who and what he was and told him to wait after the sale. He did so to his very great advantage.

This bookseller was a man named Thomas Tegg who was breaking down the old trade customs of the day. Formerly an edition was printed, sold what it could and the remainder was put in the warehouse to take its chance for the future – prices were never reduced. This man followed a contrary practice by selling off these remainders for what they would fetch. In this he was favoured by the circumstances of the times. Steam had just been introduced into the printing trade and was beginning to supersede the handpress. Steam machines must be kept going and to this end the clearance of old editions was essential.

Thomas Tegg bought up all the good standard books which publishers wanted to be freed of but did not like to sell themselves from trade pride. All kinds of library editions in 8vo and 4to from 4, 6 to 8 volumes, which sold when published at £4 or £5 were offered by Tegg for 30/- or 40/-.

This was quite revolutionary and Richard could hardly credit what he had seen and heard and when Tegg told him what he could sell to him – a bookseller – for, he was astonished that the profit was good even at those reduced prices. Richard bought £30 to £40 worth and Tegg took him home to his country house and gave him advice on what to do. They parted next day and never saw each other again, but they had many dealings over the course of years and the connection lasted until Tegg's death.

Some printing materials and a small wooden press were also bought as well as some type and binding materials. The largest of his jobbing type was a 4-line and some time after when he needed what he called a very large type for large bills, he bought a wood 11-line, second hand. It seemed to him that nothing larger could ever be required. Posters were smaller then – half sheet foolscap was general, while a demy folio was a good large size for auction bills. At Yeovil they always set up the body of an auction bill in an old pica and in that type would set up a sale bill of stock, the first item of which was 'One Thousand Sheep'. Nowadays for a sale of that size, posters 3 to 4 feet long would not be too big. It was not until 1829 that we set up our first demy bill in Lymington and it remained for many years pasted up as a triumph of skill. The first double crown was printed by us in 1832. We had by then a larger press which pulled it in two pulls and this press was in use all Richard's lifetime until his death in 1875, although we had by that time an iron press at work. Some years ago when putting in new plant we found one of the uprights and the curved crossbeam of this press in the floor of the workshop and we still preserve this as a reminder of old times.

Richard then came home and following Tegg's advice marked up his books at low figures. The townsfolk were astonished and astounded. Never before had such a thing been seen. Admiral Sir Graham Hammond passed the shop and a set of books attracted his eye. "Only so much? Are they incomplete?". "Take them home" said Richard "and if they are I will refund you the money". He bought and continued as a customer until his death in 1869.

Heavy sets which would astonish the present degenerate days were rapidly sold. Mr. Weld, the yachtsman of Pylewell, bought *Wild Sports of the West*, an enormous oblong folio, for about £7, probably published at £20 and then exchanged it for a set of *Beauties of England and Wales* of 40 volumes in 8vo, which Richard bound for him for his library. People bought largely and Tegg's sales to Richard increased and on one occasion when a £100 order was sent up, Tegg wrote to his young friend "this is something like business!" The other booksellers in the town were equally astonished and as one of them, Galpine by name, also held the post office, Richard sent up his order and money in parcels by coach in case his letters would be too closely examined.

For some time then Richard had nearly all the book trade of the town in his hands and as he was well known as a binder these sales had a double advantage as he often sold a heavy set and had the order to bind them, for cloth binding was unknown in those days and books were published only in drab paper covers. He once had an order to bind a set of large volumes for a customer who had purchased them for about 10 guineas, and who wished to take them with him by coach the next morning. He set to work by himself and got them into leather by midnight, then putting them to dry by the fire he got a little rest. Early in the morning he prepared for finishing and got them all bound and ready for the coach, taking £20 in cash. It was the same with printing. He printed Mr. Ford's Hymns all by himself, looking after the shop trade at the same time with his wife's assistance. There was not the miscellaneous business of the present day or he could not have done it.

He worked all holidays incessantly and his son Edward (my grandfather) tells how he worked with him on Good Friday all day printing tea papers, when he was so small that he and another little lad blacked 12 pulls each in turn; they were both too little to do more. He also published the various editions of the Lymington guide which were the forerunners of the history of the town later to be printed by his son. The first of these guides which I have was published in 1828. These little books were produced by setting up a few pages at a time, printing off, distributing the type and then setting up the other pages in turn. Not more than 50 sheets could have been printed in an hour by hand. How different from today when the modern high speed press can produce up to 4,000.

At this time he taught himself Latin and would study by having the grammar open on the binding press before him. At intervals he used to go up to London by coach to buy suitable books and one day went in to Bumpus' to pay a heavy bill and pulled out of his coat pocket an old wallet from which he extracted the requisite amount. When Bumpus had recovered from his surprise he advised him to beware of the acuteness of the London pickpocket.

His working day would begin with his breakfast of coffee and bread and butter with his son and an apprentice, and afterwards for five minutes he would read himself a page or two of Blair's sermons. Then to work, closing the shop like everybody else at 9 p.m. He is said to have worked like this for a month at a time without once going up the street.

Edward, the eldest son of Richard, remained at home in the business until November 1845 when he went to London but returned in December 1855 to carry on the business on the retirement of his father. He had been educated at Amsterdam House, Christchurch, and I have his copy book dated 1834. He had a great love of his native town of Lymington and over the years wrote and published the first edition of *Old Times Revisited*, 1879.

The gathering of the material to make this possible entailed an enormous amount of work and study and I understand that at one time he stayed for a week or two in a hotel near the British Museum in order to gather all available information from that quarter. He had a great gift for drawing and water colour painting and I have several of his pictures which show his skill in this direction.

In the summer of 1858 the business was moved to our present address at 105 High Street and it is interesting to record that the assessment on nos. 105 and 106 in those days was £48 gross and £40.10.0. net. The poor rate on this at 9d in the £ was 30/- for the half year and the police rate at 2½d in the £ came to 8/6d.

At this time the third town hall was still standing close against the footway in front of the shop leaving only a narrow passage for pedestrians and in consequence the shop and living quarters above must have been extremely dark. The shop was quite a small one and had been in the occupation of a Mr. West, wine merchant and private banker. The brick wine bins are still in the cellars below and family tradition says that the "strong room" was a little cupboard about 6ft. by 4ft. at the back of the shop. This was only swept away during our last extension some four years ago. Mr. West was an eccentric, having among other things built two large music rooms at the back of the premises and which as far as is known were never used. This is the building with the mansard roof which can be seen from the *Angel* yard.

The adjoining shop no. 106 was at this time occupied by a bootmaker but was soon to be thrown into the present premises. It had in the early 18th century been a chemist shop and there is some quite wonderful scroll work in gold and green behind the present ceiling paper. It was uncovered some 40 years ago but it was necessary to paper over once more. The music room then became a printing works but with the growth of business a machine shop was built immediately behind and is used as such to this day. The room thus vacated then became the composing room but by 1904 in my father's time he extended the machine room still further and the compositors were moved to the new building.

From hand press to steam machines, from steam machines to a gas engine, a huge affair with a fly wheel some 5ft high, which worked for a great number of years until the introduction of electric motors; we have thus seen all the various forms of power used in printing. Perhaps one day we shall see the introduction of a small atomic plant.

My grandfather died on 12th March 1885 at the age of 63 and the business was carried on by my father Charles and his brother Richard in partnership. This partnership continued until about 1890 when my uncle Richard, following in the footsteps of his father, moved to London and opened business not as a bookseller/printer but as a printer/publisher. The business was in Tabernacle Street and being a man of some initiative he was soon embarking on the printing and publishing of the standard works of fiction. He is reputed to have been the first man to publish a cloth bound book for a shilling and he sold these in enormous quantities. They were not well produced by comparison with those issued today by the large publishing houses, the print and paper being poor, but when one considers that they were produced before the introduction of mechanical setting it was truly a remarkable achievement.

But even in those days about 60 years ago production on such a large scale needed capital and this with the frantic cutting of wholesale prices in order to sell still larger quantities brought all his efforts to nought and the business was eventually closed down.

At the departure of my uncle to London my father was left to carry on the family business in Lymington and among other things successfully produced a second and larger edition of *Old Times Revisited*, 1900.

Another far greater effort was the publication of the *Registers of the Dutch Church of Austin Friars* in London. This enormous work was edited by Mr. Moens, of Tweed, Boldre, and consisted of some 10 or 12 volumes. Practically every surname had to be spelt when the proofs were being passed and the publication of the work was spread over many years. The earliest volume which I have is dated 1884 and we were still producing the final volume in 1912. Only a few days ago an old employee named Carter came to see me, a man in his middle 70's. He told me that he was engaged specifically for this one job and worked on it for 3½ years.

Printers at this time earned 22/- a week and worked from 7 in the morning until 7 at night but on Saturdays stopped a little earlier at 4 o'clock. On this wage a man married and brought up a family of four at the same time as buying his house on mortgage. The old fashioned word, economy, had a very real meaning in those days. What a contrast to our five days a week of 42 hours and the present wage scales.

In an old established business, owing to the change in fashion, some very odd things tend to be left by one generation to become a problem for the next. When I first entered the business one of my problems was what to do with several packing cases of envelopes, of a quite out of date size, with a very heavy black border about ½" all round. We eventually solved the problem by using them for weekly wages. One might well suppose that the effect of receiving one's wages in black bordered envelopes for 20 years would have a marked effect upon the recipients but strange to say they appeared quite unchanged.

In the course of time the business has expanded and grown out of all recognition but the same old spirit of the business remains – a family enterprise.

(A paper read to the Historical Record Society in October 1959.)

Bibliography and Further Reading

King, Richard. Round Lymington and Through the New Forest. (1828) Kings, Lymington.

King, Edward. Old Times Revisited. (1879) Kings, Lymington.

Hobby, Christopher. An Album of Old Lymington and Milford on Sea. (1989) Ensign, Southampton.

Coles, Robert. Lymington High Street Then and Now. (1984) Coles, Lymington.

Pinnell, Blake. Country House History around Lymington, Brockenhurst and Milford-on-Sea. (1987) Pinnell, Lymington.

Scene in the High Street after the 'great snowstorm' of 1881. Smith and Hidden are situated on the corner of New Lane where Boots the Chemists now stands. In the centre of the photograph is The Bugle Inn. The sign had for many years been a bull's head – the pub name being a corruption of 'bubale', a species of wild bull.

A view of the High Street from an unusual vantage point. In the left-hand corner are the premises of W. Banks, auctioneers. On the other side of the street can be seen Bailey's China and Glass Warehouse. This site is now occupied by Elliott's.